Bingham Canyon

Bingham Canyon

BY MARION DUNN

LITHOGRAPHED IN U.S.A.
PUBLISHERS PRESS
SALT LAKE CITY, UTAH

This book is proudly dedicated
to all you
Mighty Miners
wherever you are.

TABLE OF CONTENTS

ACKNOWLEDGMENTS

I LIVED IN BINGHAM CANYON from the time I was one-year-old until I went into the army early in World War II and returned often afterwards. But this history of the town could not have been written without the help of a whole lot of people.

I am deeply indebted to:

Ed W. Johnson who grew up with Bingham starting school there in 1899, in the Canyon Hall building, and who watched the town grow and then fade away. He gave freely of his time and knowledge and love of the town and was just tremendous, and I can never repay him. . . .

The four daughters of the late Mr. and Mrs. John Creedon. John Creedon kept a scrapbook on Bingham and contributed to this scrapbook with his wonderfully nostalgic column "Down Memory Lane" which ran in the *Bingham Bulletin* and was very well done. His daughters gave me full access to their father's columns and scrapbook and to you Colleen (Mrs. William May), Patsy (Mrs. Pete Massa), Mary (Mrs. George Coleman), and Michael Ann (Mrs. Dennis Scroggin), my very sincere thanks, and appreciation. . . .

Rex Tripp and his wife, the former Maisie Adderley, who contributed so much knowledge and help and who knew the town so very well. Rex Tripp was one of the men most responsible for getting the Main Street paved in Bingham in 1928. As a councilman he tackled the job that everyone said couldn't be done, and he got it done. He was just as much help to me and I thank him. . . .

Francis J. Quinn, George Dahlstrom and Everard Cowdell who took a summer evening off to talk about the early days. . . .

Lola Johanson who opened the photo files of her late husband, Dee Johanson, and furnished many of the pictures in the book. . . .

Boyd Householder, June Householder McLeod, Mrs. Edith Santistevan, Frank English, George (Brig) Knudsen and many, many others who gave photos and help. . . .

Mayor Peter C. Dimas, Councilmen Gail Farnsworth, James Xanthos and Evelyn Fontana, Clerk Mae Stillman, and the Jordan School District for making it all possible.

Bibliography

Beatrice Spendlove Bates' History of Bingham Canyon

The First Century of The Methodist Church in Utah

150 Years of Catholicity in Utah

The Bingham Bulletin

The Salt Lake Tribune

The Salt Lake Telegram

The Deseret News

Metal 1918

FOREWORD

On November 22, 1971, the town of Bingham Canyon, Utah officially ceased to exist. In truth, it had actually stopped living some years before. It had been kept legally alive only through the stubborn resistance of a few citizens and town officials who held onto their property in the face of always-increasing pressure from the mining company that had bought out their former neighbors.

When the town of Bingham Canyon passed away it had been 123 years since Thomas and Sanford Bingham drove a herd of cattle and horses to the mouth of the canyon in the Oquirrh Mountains about 28 miles southwest of Salt Lake City, Utah. The Binghams set up camp in August, 1848, and they left their family name perpetually there.

But, while the Bingham name is still remembered, the world has long forgotten why they first settled there. Because there was immense wealth in that canyon, first in timber, then in the mining of gold, silver, lead and copper ore.

It was as a mining center that Bingham first burst upon the consciousness of the region, the nation and the world. And, ironically, it was because of the wealth-giving minerals in the surrounding mountains that the town of Bingham faded away and died.

The town of Bingham Canyon never attained old age as the lives of towns are recorded. The town was incorporated in 1904, and was thus only 67 years old.

Looking back it is easy to see that Bingham was doomed almost from the beginning.

I remember a day when my brothers Albert and Jerry, our sister Betty and a friend, Rex Tripp, Jr., and I were very young. We hiked in the mountains above the town and we found a sweet spot that was seemingly isolated from civilization. It seemed to us to be miles away from the mining operation.

We spent a happy summer day there. We ran and rested on a grassy strip; we were cooled by a sweet-scented breeze; we were shaded by towering trees; we were sung to by birds of many species; we saw rabbits, porcupine, grouse and deer and wc drank from a clear, cold spring. It seemed to us as if we had discovered a secret place that would belong to us forever.

But the tenants of such ownership are shaky. The next summer we tried to return. We knew the way well. We had visited it mentally all winter. But when we climbed to the place where it should have been, it was gone. There was no grass, no trees, no wildlife. We found only railroad tracks and ugly bare rocks off which the hot sun glared cruelly.

At first we thought we had simply made a mistake and we spent the afternoon searching. But it had disappeared. On the way home we decided that it had never existed, that it had all been only a pleasant dream. Otherwise, we asked, where could it have gone?

Today, a former resident of Bingham Canyon may have the same experience by visiting the canyon. Drive up that narrow, winding road and the town is gone. There are no homes, no hotels, no rooming houses, no stores, no saloons, no businesses, no restaurants, no town hall, no Bingham Merc, no service stations, no bank, no schools, no churches.

And so, driving that street, one might ask: "Was there ever really a town here, or was it all merely a dream, a figment of the imagination?"

Know this and know this well: it was no illusion. There was such a town. Oh, yes, indeed. Once upon a time there was a Bingham Canyon, Utah.

CHAPTER ONE

THE LAST NOISY FOURTH

BEFORE THE MORNING SUN could flood over Winnamuck Cliffs the first string of firecrackers exploded. It was a series of sharp reports that sounded like small arms fire. A few seconds later it was followed by another explosion and then another until the canyon resembled a battlefield. A woman tourist from Boston was awakened in her hotel room on Main Street. She quickly got out of bed, threw a robe around her shoulders and looked out a window onto the Main Street two stories below. "You won't believe this," she told her husband. "I thought we were being attacked by outlaws, but it is only little kids with firecrackers. They aren't big enough to be playing with matches and they are setting off fireworks by themselves. I can't believe it. Someone is going to get hurt."

At exactly 9:30 A.M. the fire siren sounded. It began as a low, throaty moan, quickly rose to a tormented scream, then faded like the last wail of a dying banshee. And it set into motion a long line of people and machines that had been waiting impatiently in the tennis court-playground area of Frogtown.

At the head of the column marched the Volunteer Fire Department followed by four bands, many floats, marchers, cars, and wagons. Almost as soon as the long line started to move the breeze rippled the folds of the flags carried by the firemen. The community band and the National Guard's 222 band simultaneously swung into the stirring strains of "The Stars and Stripes Forever."

The 1936 Fourth of July parade and celebration was officially underway in Bingham Canyon, Utah.

In number of participants and the size and grandeur of the floats this would be the biggest parade yet in the town's history. Marching in the line would be the members of the Auxiliary units of the two fire departments and an item in the *Bingham Bulletin* would describe the ladies as wearing "modish bright silk shantung brightened with red buttons and belts."

Mayor John Dahlstrom and trustees John Creedon, C. A. Morley, Earl James, W. R. Sumnicht and Clerk Eugene Morris were there. The parade marshall was Salt Lake County Sheriff S. Grant Young.

Miss Virginia Harris and Miss Beth Christensen carried standards and marched in front of the Girl Scout's float. This float, colored red and green, was topped by a large replica of the scout pin and carried scouts holding placards on which the Scout Laws were printed.

Melba Nerdin, who was named "Miss Bingham" for the celebration after a contest, rode on an elaborate float. Decorated mostly in white, this float had "Miss Bingham" lettered in green along both sides. Miss Nerdin wore a summery yellow dress which was accented by rows of yellow flowers that lined the sides of the float.

One of the most attractive floats was entered by the West's Furniture Company. It was a large platform made and covered with green and yellow paper designs. It featured a number of small children including Marjorie West, Marilyn Miller, Marjorie Isbell, Donna Tibble, Richard Carter, Gwen Stokes and Loretta Robison.

The float that attracted most of the attention along the way was entered by the No. 2 Fire Department. The float's theme was safety and first aid. The department's capable first aid team of Jay Farnsworth, Tory Tobiason, Ted Robinson, Cliff Butterfield, John Hutchings and Clive Siddoway put on practical demonstrations in first aid as the float slowly made its way up the canyon. A touch of stark reality was added by equipment donated by the Bingham Hospital.

The Utah Power and Light float—its sides designed as cool-looking, blue-shadowed icebergs—was tantalizing to the crowd as it displayed numerous electrical appliances that were available that year.

The Bingham Radio shop scored a double by entering an attractive float and utilizing a loud speaker system that kept spectators and participants informed during the parade and the long day of celebrating.

There was nothing unusual about the makeup of the parade. With slight variations it could have been at home in any similar parade in any small town, anywhere. But, if the parade, itself, was not unusual, it would march through one of the most unique towns in the world.

The parade started in Frogtown. Its route took it up Main Street three miles to the Bingham Mercantile corner where it made a right turn, traveled up Carr Fork until it reached the bridge, then doubled back to the Bingham Merc where it disbanded.

A crowd packed four and six deep at some places along the way watched it pass, but it was those who watched and the town whose streets they lined that made this a parade unlike any other in the nation that day.

Because Bingham Canyon was never just another town. It was different and this difference welded its people into a oneness that was also unique in the land.

The vast majority of cities and towns in the United States have a sameness about them so that they have no personality of their own. In most towns Main Street resembles every other main street so the towns look and act alike in a dull conformity.

There are exceptions, of course. Among the larger cities, San Francisco and New Orleans have a flavor and personality all their own and are exceptions.

Among the towns of the nation, Bingham Canyon was an exception.

Bingham Canyon was a movie set come to life. It was old country and it was new.

It was sophisticated East and Wild West.

It was wood so dry it would vanish in an instant of flame. It was brick and mortar.

It was concrete and it was dirt.

It was trees and flowers and clear, cool water. It was an open sewer running down the middle of town.

It was coal and wood and cinders. And it was clear skies.

It was the thunder of blasting every day at 3 P.M. It was band concerts and community singing.

It was boys dressed in bib overalls, flannel shirts and hightop boots. It was girls with their hair cut in bangs, wearing cotton dresses and long cotton stockings.

It was the roar of the mallets hauling ore to the smelters and pouring smoke from the tunnels. It was the steady drone and the flash of sparks from the electric trains.

It was the cry of "Fire" in the night and "Play Ball" in the daytime.

It was unpainted frame houses without yards, rundown and unkempt on the outside. It was the same houses, almost dust free and immaculately clean on the inside.

It was coal-burning cooking stoves in the kitchen and pot-bellied heaters in the living room.

It was strikes and strikebreakers.

It was violence and occasional hatred. It was sympathy and charity and the "Angel of Highland Boy."

It was saloons and bars and 520 Main Street. It was churches and weddings and births and funerals.

It was gang fights in the streets. It was birthday parties and children's dances.

It was the security of couples walking down the railroad tracks in the summer evenings. It was cold, clutching fear when word spread of a bad accident on "The Hill."

It was rich and it was terribly poor.

It had characters and it had character.

It was walking to school in Highland Boy behind your dad as he broke trail through snow up to his waist. It was a boy playing in the dirt road on Heaston Heights when the spring sun melted the snow and it ran in rivulets just right to be dammed up.

It was young men coming cold and wet from the tunnels and coughing their lives away in drafty bedrooms. It was housewives hiking the canyon trails in snow and rain and mud to be beside a woman in labor.

It was a picnic in Markham Gulch. It was a mud slide down Markham Gulch.

It was old women in shawls picking up coal on the levels. It was the thrill of a first paycheck.

It was a town that was always young and healthy and seemed to be just getting started. It was a town dying without knowing it.

Bingham Canyon was a town attached to a mine. The umbilical cord was Main Street, a long, narrow, twisting thoroughfare that was simultaneously entrance and exit.

The city limits were actually four miles from the mouth of the canyon. From the city limits Main Street snaked its way up-canyon three miles to where it forked, the right road leading up Carr Fork to Highland Boy, the left continued as Main Street then covered two-and-a-half miles to Copperfield which included Dinkeyville, Telegraph, Terrace Heights, and two suburbs, known as long as the town lived, simply as Jap Camp and Greek Camp.

In the early days, Griffin House, the town's first hotel and boarding house, dominated the area where the road forked, but the area is best known to Binghamites and tourists as the Bingham Merc corner.

And up in the hills behind the Bingham Merc, spanning the mountains between Highland Boy and Copperfield and running in levels down both sides of the canyon, was the open pit copper mine that, subtly at times, with tremendous impact at others, dictated life in the shacks, shanties, homes, hotels and mansions that sheltered the town's inhabitants.

Main Street was by no means all of Bingham Canyon. The buildings of the town spread over the canyon away from Main Street and onto the very fringes and workings of the mine like barnacles on an ancient whale, but Main Street was the life line that linked town and mine.

Main Street averaged only 20 feet in width—just room enough for two cars to pass in opposite directions—and was made to seem even smaller by the buildings that lined its sides and the heavy traffic that flowed up and down reaching a peak when the shifts changed at the mines. No one who was ever trapped in his car going up the canyon while the workers just off shift were coming down, will ever forget the experience.

A young man who applied for his driver's license at the Utah State Capitol in Salt Lake City in 1940, was asked by the examiner, "Do you drive in Bingham Canyon all the time?" The answer was "Yes," and the examiner told the applicant not to start the car, he had passed. "If you can drive in Bingham Canyon, you can drive anyplace in the world," he explained.

It was up that narrow Main Street the Fourth of July parade would travel. As the marchers moved out the warm breeze carried the scent of elderberries, choke cherries, wild flowers, and trees that promised a warm summer day ahead. It was a holiday so the huge mine was silent, the electric trains and shovels idle on the tracks and in the mounds of waste and ore. But there was noise and confusion all along the way. Firecrackers exploded. Cap guns were fired. Children ran and played and called and waved to participants in the parade. The four bands played, sometimes in unison and sometimes separately, along the way. Dogs barked. Relatives and friends applauded. And all along the way hawkers tried to talk passerbys into buying whatever they had to sell—peanuts, popcorn, candy, fireworks, souvenirs, ice cream, cold drinks—or to urge them to try the rides and games that were available.

This, then, was the Bingham Canyon through which the parade would pass:

FROGTOWN

While the parade organized and began at the playground, Frogtown proper started a few hundred yards farther down the canyon, just before the city limits where the slag dump and the smokestacks of the old Yampa Smelter on the right, and the Bourgard slaughterhouse on the left, were well-known landmarks.

Another familiar landmark near the city limits was the dirt road gouged into the left side of the mountain. This was the "Damn Fool Road" and led only to the "Damn Fool Tunnel" which got its name from the old-timers who said it was so dangerous only a newcomer down on his luck or a damn fool would work there.

Frogtown was different in that it not only was split into right and left sides by the Main Street, but it was farther divided by the railroad tracks on the left side of the canyon.

Going up the canyon on the right side, Frogtown included the big, red frame house that once was the home of the smelter superintendent, and was reached by a long flight of stairs; the Amicone Bar, a Standard Service station and bulk plant, the Panos Apartments, Wolfe's yard that stretched up the hillside then dipped downhill to the Moonlight Gardens, Tom Praggastis store, the Liberty Bell Bakery, a pool hall, a row of homes called Praggastis Row, and Dimitri Bakery.

A driveway led back to Mayne's yard. Frank Miller had a laundry warehouse and then came a section of residences belonging to some of the town's pioneer families, the Tibbles, Grants, Wests and Longfellows. Near them was an automobile repair shop operated by Adderley and Nichols who had a service station on the other side of the street just below the playground. The Furgis family had once owned a service station in that locality but now had the Furgis Apartments which were above Christ Apostol's grocery and meat market and the Spanos barber shop. From there residences lined both sides of Main Street past the start of Railroad Avenue, up to the Royal Laundry, Charley Dimas' Bingham Grocery Number 1 and Dixon Gulch.

The left side of Frogtown contained the long-time business residence of the Citizen's Coal and Supply Company, the Evans Ice Company, two breweries, Adderley and Nichols station, and on the left side of the tracks, houses and Frank

Shafter's store, then more houses and the tennis court and playground.

Most residents of Frogtown can remember only one time when there was a net strung across the fenced-in tennis court. It was used more often as a roller skating rink and at least once was flooded in the winter and used for ice skating.

The playground, a wide stretch of yellow-colored dirt resembling a mine dump, once held the tram houses for the cable buckets that carried ore down the canyon to be loaded on train cars and carried to the smelters.

A once-new set of swings were in disrepair and there was a slide that was ripped on the bottom and required deft maneuvering for a safe and fun slide.

RAILROAD AVENUE

Frogtown ended as Main Street curved left just up-canyon from Christ's Meat and Grocery store. Branching off to the left of Main Street was a separate road and was named Railroad Avenue.

From the earliest days of the camp until the automobile became the chief means of transportation, Railroad Avenue was actually the Main Street.

There was good reason for this. The railroad linked Bingham Canyon with the outside world and the D&RG had a depot there where the passenger trains disembarked their loads daily. From there travelers continued uptown by stage coach or horse and buggy or simply walked to their destination.

The Bingham Dairy was on the border of Frogtown and Railroad Avenue. Ross Marriott had a blacksmith shop and livery stable there. Mr. Devore, a tall, skinny gentleman who had a southern charm, but had fought for the Union in the Civil War and remembered Abraham Lincoln, owned a row of garages which he rented to car owners and he lived in a frame house near the garages.

Flora Amicone lived in a house that was far up the canyon wall and was reached by climbing a flight of wooden steps. There was Tuft's and Ross Cushing's Coal Yard, the Alexander Apartments, Prigmore's Coal Yard and then Chandler's Bingham Lumber and Coal Yard up to the far end where the road turned right and re-joined Main Street just across the street from the Number 2 Fire Department.

DIXON GULCH, HEGLAND ALLEY, FREEMAN GULCH

Across the street from the Royal Laundry and Bingham Grocery Number 1, the road branched to the right involving three parts of the town spanning a few hundred feet in length.

These areas were Dixon Gulch, Hegland Alley and Freeman Gulch.

Dixon Gulch ran up to Freeman Gulch and Hegland Alley ran adjacent to Main Street and connected to Dixon and Freeman gulches.

Hegland Alley was the home of many of the town's pioneer families and one of these, George Chandler, owned what could be rightfully called a mansion. Later it became the Cook Apartments.

The Chandler house fronted on Main Street looking across to Railroad Avenue and its back yard was on Hegland Alley. The Chandlers had a neat, well-kept lawn and garden and to keep the neighborhood children from trespassing, built a long stone wall the length of the yard. Still, the children would climb the fence to retrieve a stray ball or just to enjoy the luxury of a lawn. So, wooden pickets were placed on top of the stone wall, then strands of wire, and at one time the tops of the pickets were covered with a sticky tar.

It didn't completely shut the children out. Boys still scaled the fence, but it did limit the view. Few people, children or adults, walked down Hegland Alley without peeking at the Chandler's yard.

The main road up Freeman Gulch came almost in the middle of a sharp bend in Main Street. The Freeman Road climbed steeply up the gulch to a flat stretch of ground partway up the hill. At the south end of this flat was the Tom Masters home, a large, frame house with a wide, covered porch that was reached, like so many of the better homes in the canyon, by a long flight of wooden stairs.

Then the road continued up the gulch past wooden houses until it ended short of the mine where, in the early days three Freeman brothers were killed in a cave-in.

Back on Main Street, the Number 2 Fire Station was located just above Freeman Gulch. On the hill behind the station was the fire siren mounted on the top of a metal, scaffold-like structure. Once a fire bell had hung there, but it was replaced by the more efficient—and frightening—fire siren.

Main Street made an S curve here and was residential for a stretch, with homes on both sides and with an area known as Heaston Heights on the hillside on the right of the canyon.

HEASTON HEIGHTS

There was only one dirt road leading to and from Heaston Heights. It branched off Main Street, doubled back toward the canyon's mouth, up a steep hill to the top of the heights where it ended abruptly. A foot path continued around the side of the mountain to Freeman Gulch.

One of the main features of Heaston Heights was a huge rock that rose from the canyon floor. Joe Kemp and his family lived in a house on the top of the rock, most of the rock serving as a back yard and garden.

Rex Tripp, one of the officers of the Bingham Mercantile Company and long-time civic leader, had another of the impressive homes on Heaston Heights.

The Tripp home was on the mountain side of the Heaston Heights road, at the south end. It had a wide porch and looked down on two views of the canyon road.

Ross Hocking, another pioneer, lived in a neat frame home behind the Tripp residence and the Church of Jesus Christ of Latter-day Saints ward house was built along the side of the canyon as a neighbor to the Hocking's residence.

BACK TO MAIN

Main Street was residences and apartments, including two show places, one owned by Adolph Chiara and the other by the Contratto family. A service station was on the right and on the left a grocery store originally Lott's Grocery, then Dowd's Cash Grocery, was the last building for a long stretch. A cribbing held back the mountain on the left side and ran from the sidewalk high up the canyon wall.

Two school buildings were on the right side. These had served in several capacities, first as high school and elementary, then as elementary and then were left vacant.

The first of these was remodeled and became the American Legion Civic Center, officially opening in this capacity on Saturday, April 21, 1935. The first event that night was billed as an "Athletic Carnival" with an all-star boxing and wrestling card held in the old high school gym. It was sponsored by Bingham Post Number 30, American Legion and was called "The Greatest Exhibition ever held in Bingham" and tickets cost $1.00.

The school-building-Civic-Center would remain, but the other school building there would be razed.

After the stretch of cribbing on the left of the street, there were homes and a bottling works in McGuire Gulch and at the head of the gulch was the Community Church, a large, white frame building.

The Community Church originally was in Carr Fork, but since it also served as a school and was located near saloons, it was moved down the canyon. It was one of the early school houses as well as a church.

Bingham Central had been the high school, but became the elementary school when the new high school was built in Copperton in the early 1930's.

The school ground had slides, swings, tricky bars and a home for the principal was on the grounds.

The old Red Wing Mill stood just above the school and was there long after it ceased to operate. After it was dismantled in the early 1930's, the Bingham Grocery Number 2 or Chipian's was built on Main Street there and the rest of the property became part of the school's playground.

MARKHAM GULCH

Markham Gulch, at one time one of the area's most picturesque spots, was across the street from Bingham Central and was easily marked by the 200 foot high Markham Bridge that spanned it.

One of the town's most famous buildings, Canyon Hall, was on the right side of the street at the head of Markham

Gulch. A huge frame structure, Canyon Hall was a social center serving as roller skating rink, a dance hall, meeting place and schoolhouse.

The Canyon Hall had a spring floor, the first of its kind in Utah, and this added a new dimension to dancing, skating or just walking.

Spud Morley's Canyon Garage was in the lower part of the building.

MAIN STREET TO THE FORKS

Among the homes on Main Street above Markham Gulch were those belonging to Charles Adderley, pioneer businessman and president of the Bingham Mercantile Company, and theater owner Harold Chesler.

The old Union Hall, built by early union men, was now an apartment on the left side of the street and just above it was an apartment house that had once been the site of a livery stable and had housed the post office.

Then came the Bingham Garage owned by Chick Adderley and Ren Nichols and this marked the beginning of the town's main business district.

If nothing else, the Bingham Garage was recognition of the fact the automobile had replaced the horse in the canyon. Chick Adderley and Ren Nichols opened the garage on October 6, 1920. It had a basement parking lot with a ramp for cars on the lower end and a wooden stairway on the other end. The main garage was on ground level and there were additional parking stalls upstairs.

A road ran through a small tunnel on the lower end of the garage and led to the Utah Power and Light substation.

The Bingham Garage also marked the start of the town's main business district. Before the big fire of 1924, the Bourgard butcher shop, at its time the most modern of establishments, and the famous Bingham Hotel were among the buildings just above the garage. But that fire destroyed a whole section of town including the two landmarks.

Now the new post office was there and was already three years old. Across the street was the Utah Copper Hospital where Doctors R. G. Frazier and H. C. Jenkins had their offices and a dentist, Dr. B. D. Bennion, had an upstairs office.

From here on the canyon was extremely narrow and it was heavily populated with businesses, hotels, apartments and homes lined up side by side and stacked on top of each other.

The most famous of the buildings, perhaps, was the Bourgard Apartments on the right side of the street. Owned by Jerome Bourgard, a pioneer businessman, the building was constructed in 1914, by one of Bingham's leading carpenters and architects, Leonard Porter.

The top three floors were apartments, each with a front porch overlooking the street. The ground floor held many business establishments over the years including doctors offices and mortuaries.

As the Fourth of July parade moved through this section, the porches of the apartment units were filled with the tenants and their friends enjoying a grandstand view of the proceedings.

Wilford Harris and his family had a small home by the apartments that was also a landmark for years.

Going up Main Street after the Post Office on the left and the Utah Copper Hospital on the right, were the Wells Grocery and Apartments, Sturm's Cafe, Utah Power and Light, Bogan Hardware, Dr. Paul Richard's home, Bingham Meat and the Mascot Apartments, The Bingham Bulletin, Bingham Drug, Berg's Bingham Furniture, Bingham Radio, the Bingham Hospital headed by Dr. Richards and one of the finest in the region; Social Hall (once the Gem Theater), the Number 1 Fire Station, a Rexall Drug Store, a clothing store, a photography shop, M. L. James, Royal Candy Number 1, J. C. Penney's, Bert Thaxton's barber shop, the bank, the Royal Chocolate Shop, the Princess Theater and the apartments, the Pastime, the Copper King, City Hall, the Bingham Mercantile Company, the Belmont Hotel, the Knight Hotel, Butte Club, the Bingham Stage Lines, the Telephone Company, apartment houses, the Canyon Bar, the Vietti Grocery, the old California Hotel, and one of the best known addresses in town, 520 Main.

CARR FORK

In front of the Bingham Mercantile Company, the road forked and the parade moved up the right hand fork, Carr Fork.

There was an Italian-French Cafe which later moved down Main Street; Goris' Barber Shop with its row of chairs; the Carr Fork garage with its ramp leading to the upstairs parking, the apartment houses with the wooden porches, the alley leading to a bar, the George Klonizos Barber Shop where the owner was a familiar figure every Sunday as he washed and polished his Graham Page automobile in the street there as a regular weekly ritual; a boarding house, the Seminole Hotel, the Canyon Market, houses, the alley that was used as a short cut to Copper Heights and Upper Main Street, the Catholic Church, boarding houses, individual homes, a storage garage, the big, brick Penny Apartments, the Tram, Gemmell Club, Cyprus Hall, three brick bungalows, the Swedish Zion Lutheran Church, the Carr Fork Bridge and more homes and garages.

COPPER HEIGHTS

Copper Heights was a promontory overlooking the canyon where some of the Utah Copper Mine executives had their homes. It was reached by a road from the mine property and by a long flight of wooden stairs from Carr Fork.

HIGHLAND BOY

The Parade disbanded after turning around at the Carr Fork Bridge and marching back to the Bingham Merc corner.

But that was not the end of the canyon.

Had it continued up the right fork it would have reached the Highland Boy area of the canyon.

The first area of Highland Boy was known as Phoenix.

The canyon was nearing its highest point here and was naturally narrow and confined. Moving up the area were parts of Highland Boy respectively known as Phoenix, Yampa, Doty Gulch, Highland Boy Flats, then Frisco and the Boston Con. The best known building in the area was the Community House run by Ada Duhigg, "The Angel of Highland Boy."

At the very top, the Boston Con was on the left side of the canyon and the Frisco was on the right side.

COPPERFIELD

Located two-and-one-half miles farther up Main Street was Copperfield or Upper Bingham. Before the vehicular tunnel through the mountains was completed in 1938, the road to Copperfield was a continuation of Main Street.

Along the way were several small bridges and the famous E-line bridge. There were safety sheds erected to protect cars and pedestrians from falling rocks while blasting was underway in the open cut mine.

The big Rex Hotel was a familiar landmark just inside Copperfield and there were numerous businesses, hotels, boarding houses and bars. The Lendaris Market and Miner's Merc were well known along with the U.S. Hotel and boarding house. There was the Copperfield School and the Copper field Theater.

Included in the Copperfield region were Dinkeyville, Telegraph, Terrace Heights, Jap Camp, Greek Camp, and at the highest point on the main line of the canyon, Galena, where ore was first discovered in 1863.

FUN AND GAMES

The parade ended after traveling almost the entire length of the town, but the Fourth of July celebration was just beginning.

The business district was a jammed mass of humanity as the parade broke up. The people had come from Copperfield, Highland Boy, Copperton, Lead Mine and Lark as well as Bingham proper. Others had come from points around the valley and state and there were many tourists who happened to be there to see the town and the mine.

After the parade ended the crowd jammed into the Princess Theater for the annual program.

The program began with the crowd standing and singing, "America." Councilman W. R. Sumnicht gave a short welcoming speech. Rex Tripp Jr. played a trumpet solo and Eldon Tuft sang a vocal solo. Congressman J. Will Robinson gave a patriotic speech and Arlene Erickson played an accordion solo. Sheriff Young talked, praising the townspeople for the enthusiasm shown in the celebration and urging them to continue their efforts. Then John Creedon presented the Miss Bingham awards to Melba Nerdin, Jenean Almonetti, Pat Doyle, Mildred Jumper, Arlene Erickson, Mary Bradley and Emma Evankovich. The orchestra played The National

Anthem while the audience sang under the direction of Mrs. D. N. Larson, and the program was over.

The celebration moved back to the narrow street. In the time left before noon, races were held in the street for children.

Boys and girls up to five years of age raced and each entrant was given 25 cents. Then by ages, boys and girls up to nine years of age raced with first place in each age and division winning 40 cents, second 30 cents, third and fourth 20 cents each.

After the children's races, the tempo slacked for awhile as the people went home or to one of the cafes for lunch.

At 1:30 P.M. the older boys and girls raced for money. The races were held on the upper Main Street in front of City Hall and the Bingham Merc.

While the races were going on, a band concert was held on the Bingham Merc porch.

At 2:00 P.M. a dance for boys and girls up to 14 years old, was held at the Civic Center and after the dance the youngsters were given free ice cream and popcorn.

Shortly before 4:30 P.M. a mass exodus took place, people left Bingham Canyon in a train of automobiles. They went down the canyon, past Dry Fork and the English Dairy, past Lead Mine and the precipitation plant, and up into Copperton where they turned into the parking lot across from the high school and beside the Copper Baseball Park.

Gemmell Club, the Utah Copper Company's semipro entry in the Industrial League, was to meet Provo in the second game of a doubleheader.

In the first game, played at Provo, the Provo team beat Gemmell Club, 6-5, and the Bingham fans were anxious to cheer their favorites to a win in the second game scheduled for 5:00 P.M. in the Copper Park.

In the game, Gemmell Club won, 10-2. The victory made the drive back up the canyon a happy trip.

Bingham Canyon's officials had urged people not to use personal fireworks to make the holiday a safer one and for the first time put on a public fireworks exhibition. It started at 8:30 P.M. and was held on the B&G Point across from the Federal Building. It was a success but it did little to stop individuals who still held their own fireworks shows in front of their homes so the entire canyon was a fireworks exhibition.

At 9:30 P.M. men and women, in couples and stag, converged on the Civic Center for the Grand Ball. Admission was 50 cents and ladies were free and by 10:00 P.M. the old high school gym was jammed with dancing couples.

Not everyone attended the dance. Some residents sat on their front porches listening to the radio and watching children light sparklers, firecrackers and other fireworks including Roman Candles. Some played cards with friends or relatives and so the night passed swiftly.

Shortly before 1:00 A.M. in the Civic Center the orchestra played the traditional "Good Night Ladies" while the swaying couples danced close to each other and many kissed in the darkened room.

Then the music ended. The lights came on full. The orchestra members hurriedly packed their instruments and left. The couples went hand in hand down the long stairway and into the cool canyon morning.

The 1936 Fourth of July celebration officially ended in Bingham Canyon.

It was a quiet ending to what had been a boisterous day. All day long the town's children had littered the street with firecrackers. Lighted firecrackers were tossed into the street, they were thrown from open upstairs windows and thrown from rooftops.

The tourists from Boston had been stunned by what they saw and heard and the man said: "I am surprised and shocked at the freedom you people allow your children. This is the first time I have ever witnessed a really noisy Fourth of July when kids could shoot off all the fireworks they wanted."

It had been a noisy Fourth, but it was history, now, and it would fade into history like so many other traditions.

It was the last really noisy Fourth of July in Bingham Canyon. The next year use of individual fireworks was banned and it became illegal to own firecrackers.

CHAPTER TWO

ALMOST BORN ON A MOUNTAINTOP

HE WAS ALMOST BORN on the top of the mountain which was the highest point of the main canyon, but in the end he wasn't born in Bingham Canyon at all, but at 7th East and 5th South in Salt Lake City, Utah.

In the late winter of 1893, a miner named George Johnson and his wife Matilda, were expecting a child at anytime. George was working in the South Galena tunnel and they lived in a small, wooden cabin there at the very tip of the Copperfield region of Bingham Canyon.

There was a lot of snow in late February and always the threat of more. The wind whipped the snow in flurries around the cabin and the entrance to the South Galena. The Johnsons had intended to have the baby in the cabin, but as the month moved on, and the snow stayed deep, they began to worry. There was only one doctor in the region and if a snowstorm hit the area when the baby decided to make his appearance, well, George didn't like the idea of being snow-bound at that time and Matilda worried, too. So, at the end of the month George and Matilda left the cabin at Galena, went down the canyon, across the flats and to Salt Lake City.

There, in a house at about 7th East and 5th South, with the help of a mid-wife, a son was born to the Johnsons on March 3. They named him Edwin.

When George and Matilda Johnson took their new son back to the shack at South Galena in March of 1893, Bingham Canyon had already been a mining center for 30 years (credit for the discovery of ore there has generally been accepted as September 17, 1863) and it would be 11 more years before the camp incorporated and became a town. And, as in the rest of America in the eighteen-sixties, 'seventies, 'eighties and 'nineties, it was a time of ferment and discontent.

It was the time when William Vanderbilt, son of the old commodore, said in New York, "The public be damned." And for many that became the password to success.

It was the time of the few very rich and the very many terribly poor. It was a time when men toiled in the wet and darkness of the mines without safety and health regulations. It was a time when the seeds were planted that would bring to Bingham Canyon the violence and bitter strikes of the 1900's.

But it was also a time of progress and great promise.

It was the time of the electric light and the telephone and soon it would be the time of the automobile.

It was a time when many men looked at Bingham Canyon, not as a source of great wealth, but as a place to build a town and establish a home.

In 1893, it had been two years since the *Bingham Bulletin* printed its first issue on July 5, 1891, and there were already many established business and professional men in town.

The Griffin Hotel stood at the junction of Carr Fork and Main where the Bingham Mercantile Company would later be established. Jerome Bourgard built a two-story building next to the Barney Quinn building above the junction of Carr Fork and Main, directly opposite Fritz Miller's Social Hall that year. But, where there were sidewalks they were wooden and the creek that ran down the center of the town was an open sewer.

It was estimated at the time there were about 1,500 people in the Bingham Canyon area. People crowded the one-way street backing up when occasionally a horse drawn carriage or wagon blocked the way. The canyon was alive with sounds. There was the swish-swish of women's skirts sweeping the wooden sidewalks. There was the rumble as a 6-horse ore, beer or freight wagon went by. Men called to each other from the doors of saloons.

Many smells filled the air. There was the smell of fish, fried meat, cooking vegetables, horse manure, dogs, dust and smoke. Oddly, there was no stench from the sewer, a fact attributed by medical men to the copper in the water serving as a deodorizing and bacteria-killing agent.

And to many men it was the smell and sound of home. These men wanted a town and the security that goes with local government—fire and police protection, judicial service, and the commerce and comfort the times would allow. Some of the men who would one day direct the town's affairs, like Ed Johnson, were at that time mere babies or young boys. But when they were ready to serve, they would have a town waiting for them.

As early as February 4, 1871, the residents of the Bingham area had been organized into a county voting precinct and helped elect Salt Lake County officials and a local constable.

But as the century turned that was not enough. In 1901, it was obvious to the people in the canyon they needed better fire protection and that water and sanitation facilities would have to be provided. So, business and community leaders banded together and launched a drive to organize a local government.

In 1904, Bingham Canyon incorporated and became a town. The Salt Lake County Commission appointed a town board to serve for one year when a municipal election would be held to name a board of and by the people.

Appointed to the first board were A. V. Anderson who was named president of the board, and trustees Charles E. Adderley, Jerome Bourgard, Charles Brink and William Waters with Francis W. Quinn to serve as town clerk.

On February 29, 1904, the board met for the first time. It was a busy meeting. In addition to setting salaries for the town clerk (Mr. Quinn), treasurer (Mr. Adderley), and the public health officer (Dr. Smedley), liquor and trade licenses were approved and areas of taxation were established.

Bingham Canyon was in its own hands.

Time was to prove they were capable hands.

In 1914, the City Hall was finished and from then until the end the two story brick building located on Main Street across from the Bingham Merc, was the scene of almost all important decisions concerning the town and its affairs.

A mayor and board of trustees were elected every two years and most of the campaigns were hotly contested, but were conducted on a high level.

The list of mayors and trustees of Bingham Canyon is an impressive one. Several mayors served more than one term and all seem to have discharged their duties well.

By years, the mayors, councilmen and town clerks were:

1904—President, A. V. Anderson; trustees, C. E. Adderley, Jerome Bourgard, Charles Brink, William B. Waters; clerk, Francis W. Quinn.

1906—President, Anton Christensen; trustees, C. E. Adderley, A. G. Gabrielson, John G. Hocking, James P. Motherwell; clerk, Charles Heberer.

1908—President, Thomas H. Quillan; trustees, Al Osborne, Jerome Bourgard, Jr., V. B. Jones, A. G. Gabrielson; clerk, F. W. Quinn.

1910—President, Thomas H. Quillen; trustees, C. E. Adderley, H. S. Brownlee, Jerome Bourgard, Jr., William B. Waters; clerk, F. W. Quinn.

1912—President, Thomas H. Quillen; trustees, C. E. Adderley, H. S. Brownlee, A. G. Gabrielsen, R. A. Greer; clerk, F. W. Quinn.

1914—President, Dr. F. E. Straup; trustees, Samuel Byram, Willard V. Evans, Stephan J. Hays, Stanley Johns; clerk, C. L. Countryman.

1916—President, Q. B. Kelly; trustees, C. E. Adderley, H. S. Brownlee, S. L. Byram, T. B. Stephens; clerk, F. W. Quinn.

1918—Same as 1916.

1919—President, C. E. Adderley; trustees, I. M. Gauchet, John W. Contratto; clerk, F. W. Quinn.

1920—President, C. E. Adderley; trustees, Dr. J. F. Flynn, Peter Service, D. W. Coakley, Dan Fitzgerald; clerk, F. W. Quinn.

1922—President, Dr. F. E. Straup; trustees, James A. Wright, Boyd J. Bernard, Dan Fitzgerald, Ray H. Kenner; clerk, F. W. Quinn.

1924—President, Dr. F. E. Straup; trustees, Boyd J. Bernard, Dan Fitzgerald, Ray H. Kenner, J. A. Wright; clerks, F. W. Quinn, A. J. Sorenson.

1926—President, Dr. F. E. Straup; trustees, Dan Fitzgerald, Ray H. Kenner, Dominic Pezzopane, A. J. Sorenson; clerk, F. W. Quinn.

1928—President, Dr. J. F. Flynn; trustees, Thomas McMullen, Austin Larick, John West, James Nerdin, Mrs. Mary E. Nerdin; clerk, F. W. Quinn.

1930—President, Dr. J. F. Flynn; trustees, A. C. Larick, T. H. McMullen, John T. West, Rex Tripp; clerk, C. L. Countryman.

1931—Trustee, Clive Siddoway; clerk, John T. West.

1932—President, H. S. Brownlee; trustees, A. C. Larick, Rex T. Tripp, R. R. Marriott, W. R. Sumnicht, John E. Dahlstrom, Ed Johnson, F. W. Quinn; clerk, Eugene Morris.

1934—President, John E. Dahlstrom; trustees, Ed Johnson, C. A. Morley, F. W. Quinn, W. R. Sumnicht; clerk, Eugene Morris.

1936—President, John E. Dahlstrom; trustees, John J. Creedon, Earl James, C. A. Morley, W. R. Sumnicht; clerk, Eugene Morris.

1938—(Became a third class city). Mayor, Ed Johnson; councilmen, A. J. Ablett, R. D. Johnston, C. A. Morley, A. J. Sorenson; recorder, Eugene Morris.

1940—Mayor, Ed Johnson; councilmen, A. J. Sorenson, A. J. Ablett, R. D. Johnston, C. A. Morley, F. W. Quinn; clerk recorders, Eugene Morris, Chris Praggastis.

1944—Mayor, R. A. Murano; councilmen, A. J. Chipian, Ross Cushing, C. L. Johnson, Ken Shulsen; recorders, Eugene Morris, F. W. Quinn, Harvey Wolfe.

1946—Mayor, Dale Johnston; councilmen, John W. Holmes, Anast J. Chipian, Bob Jimas, Elmo Nelson; recorder, Eugene Morris.

1948—Mayor, R. A. Murano; councilmen, G. L. West, Ross Cushing, F. J. Quinn, Harold Chesler; recorder, Eugene Morris.

1950—Mayor, C. A. Morley; councilmen, Harley English, Elmo Nelson, Joe Dispenza, Leonard Miller; recorder, Eugene Morris.

1952—Mayor, C. A. Morley; councilmen, G. L. West, Joseph Timothy, Joseph Dispenza, Marlin Schultz, Bob Jimas; recorder, Eugene Morris.

1954—Mayor, Joe Dispenza; councilmen, Marlin Schultz, Ross Cushing, Joseph Timothy, Bob Jimas; recorder, Eugene Morris.

1956—Mayor, Joe Dispenza; councilmen, Ross Cushing, Marlin Schultz, G. L. West, Bob Jimas, R. A. Murano; recorder, Eugene Morris.

1957—Mayor, Joe Dispenza; councilmen, R. A. Murano, Peter Dimas, Harold Chesler, F. J. Quinn, Bob Jimas, Marlin Schultz; recorder, Eugene Morris, Mae Stillman.

1958—Mayor, Joe Dispenza; councilman, F. L. West, Peter Dimas, F. J. Quinn, Verl Peterson; recorder, Mae Stillman.

1960—Mayor, Joe Dispenza; councilmen, Verl Peterson-G. L. West, Ross Cushing, Peter Dimas, F. J. Quinn; recorder, Mae Stillman.

1961—Mayor, Joe Dispenza; councilmen, G. L. West, Ross Cushing, Peter Dimas, F. J. Quinn, Walter Swenson, Gail Farnsworth; recorder, Mae Stillman.

1962—Mayor, Peter C. Dimas; councilmen, Gail Farnsworth, Evelyn Fontana, W. W. Raby, Walter Swenson; recorder, Mae Stillman.

1962—Councilwoman, Edith Scussel.

1964—Mayor, Peter Dimas; councilmen, Walter Swenson, Gail Farnsworth, Evelyn Fontana, Hunt Nielson, David Dimmick; recorder, Mae Stillman.

1965—Mayor, Peter Dimas; councilmen, Evelyn Fontana, Walter Swenson, Gail Farnsworth, David Dimmick, Hunt L. Nielson; recorder, Mae Stillman.

1967—Mayor, Peter Dimas; councilmen, Evelyn Fontana, Walter Swenson, Gail Farnsworth, Hunt L. Nielson; recorder, Mae Stillman.

1969—Mayor, Peter Dimas; councilmen, Evelyn Fontana, Gail Farnsworth, James Xanthos; recorder, Mae Stillman.

It is a measure of the town that the problems that faced the first board in 1904, were the same as those that faced almost every administration. These were: fire protection, water, and sewage disposal.

On May 2, 1905, a special bond election authorized bonding indebtedness for $10,000 to establish a water system. George E. Chandler, a Bingham banker, had his bid for a bond issue bearing six percent interest accepted and a sinking fund was created for redemption of the bonds.

Water was always a problem in the canyon. It is ironic that one of the main sources of water for the town was part of the canyon two miles below the city limits called Dry Fork. Water was carried by wagon from Dry Fork and sold in town.

Another early source of water was from men who filled two five gallon cans of water at springs, and carried them on yokes to houses in the neighborhood. For awhile there was a well on main street above the Bourgard Apartments and there were water tanks at Markham, Heaston and Adderley's.

The first big water project was in 1918, when a tunnel was dug from Dry Fork and water was piped through it to the town.

When the water system was installed the plans were somehow destroyed and there was only one man, Fay Mitchell, assistant water superintendent, who had memorized the location of the valves. So Fay had a lifetime job. He was one of the canyon's familiar figures as—dressed in khaki shirt and trousers, the pant legs rolled up over hightop boots, and chewing on a cigar—he went about his duties.

In the late 1930's larger pipes were laid and the WPA manned the last big tunnel job for the water system.

Bingham's second town board, and its first elected body, was named in a municipal election on November 7, 1905. Anton Christensen was elected President of the Board with C. E. Adderley, A. G. Gabrielson, John Hocking and Eli Mitchell elected as trustees. F. W. Quinn was reappointed as town clerk.

It would take time and much money but the new town tackled its fire fighting problems.

In the early days church bells were used as the fire alarms and men would man bucket brigades to combat the blaze. The line would form at the creek and run to the property on fire. The men would pass full buckets up from the creek and the empty ones back to be refilled.

In April of 1905, a fire alarm system was installed and spools of fire hose were purchased. Two years later, in October, 1907, the town board approved the organization of a fire department with the business community donating money to be used for this purpose.

Fire units Number One and Number Two were formed. Each unit was to have 50 volunteer firemen with a chief in charge of each company. Fire Company Number 1 had under its control all the town from Bingham Central School (across the street from Markham Gulch) south, or up the canyon. Number 2 was in charge of the town from the school north, or down the canyon.

In case of fire, the department was given the right of way on the street and each chief was given authority of a police officer until an officer could arrive on the scene.

In May of 1910, the town board created fire inspection districts and the office of fire inspector. In 1911, the fire alarm system was improved again with purchase and installation of two automatic bellstriches which cost $975.

Fire Hall Number 1, in the main business district of Bingham, was the first station built, and the Number 2 hall was built just above Freeman Gulch across the street from the point where Railroad Avenue joined Main Street. Funds to build the Number 2 hall came from a bond election.

Over the years new equipment was added regularly, fire sirens replaced the bells and serving in the volunteer fire department was a badge of honor. The Bingham units were the equal of any in the state.

Before the automobile became popular the streets were unpaved and this was satisfactory. But as the automobile became the chief means of transportation the city was faced with the problem of paving its street.

This was done in 1928

The sewer was something else again but in the early 1930's, the open sewer that ran the length of the canyon was covered and in itself this was unique. The unusual topography of the town enabled part of the concrete flume to be used as a sidewalk in many places. Removable gratings were placed at intervals permitting the city snow plow to dispose of the snow as it kept the street open in stormy weather. The sewer served as a storm sewer and in case of bad fires where there was also a shortage of water, the sewer water was dammed off and pumped into service.

The sewer was built as a WPA project and, despite its importance to the community, became a trouble spot. Because of WPA regulations, many of the workers on the project were hired from the Magna area although there were plenty of unemployed men in Bingham who wanted the work.

It took time, effort and money, but one-by-one Bingham licked its municipal problems.

Contrary to the town's reputation as a rough and tumble mining camp, crime was never a real problem. Atha Williams was the town's first sheriff and is remembered as a man of small stature but big in nerve.

The jailhouse was in the City Hall and most of its residents were there on charges of being drunk in public. They were kept overnight or until they sobered up and then released.

There was one inmate, however, who took a long time getting over his spree. He was drunk for several days and the police couldn't understand this because he had no visitors nor any visible source of alcohol.

Yet, each morning he was as drunk as the night he was arrested.

The case was never officially solved. Finally he woke up with a hangover and was released. But the answer was simple. After dark each night one of his friends would sneak up to the large window outside the cell that was covered with a heavy wire screen. There was a tiny hole in the screen and the man on the outside would stick a straw in a fifth of whiskey, hold it high over his head and push the other end of the straw through the hole in the screen. The inside man simply sipped the whiskey through the straw to prolong his mystifying bender.

Bingham Canyon had crime, of course. Its most notorious one came in 1913, and involved a young miner named Rafael Lopez.

Every person who lived in Bingham Canyon from that year until the end has heard the story of Lopez and been intrigued with the question of what happened to him.

On November 21, 1913, Lopez shot and killed another miner named Juan Valdez. After the shooting, Lopez went to his cabin where he took his rifle and some shells and headed over the mountains toward Lehi.

At about 3:30 P.M. the next day four officers of the law, County Sheriffs Julius Sorensen, Otto Whitbeck and Nephi Jensen, and Bingham Chief of Police, William J. "Bill" Grant, approached the ranch house of Edward B. Jones about four miles north of Pelican Point and nine miles west of Lehi. They had tracked Lopez to that point and had reason to believe he might be in the house.

Sorensen and Whitbeck rode up to the house while Grant and Jensen remained about 300 yards from the house. Suddenly two shots were fired and Grant and Jensen fell. The other two officers hurried back to the downed men. Here another shot dropped Whitbeck from his saddle. Sorensen leaped off his horse and returned the fire. He claimed to have seen Lopez clearly, but there were no answering shots.

Grant, Whitbeck and Jensen died and now Lopez was wanted for four murders.

Posses were formed and the hunt continued in the Lehi area for several days then turned back to Bingham Canyon where the people were fully aroused. Grant had been Bingham's second police chief succeeding Atha Williams. He was in his third term and was highly respected. His murder stirred the town into action.

In the canyon, Lopez went to the shack of a former friend, Mike Stefano, who lived in one of the Apex shacks near the Number 2 tunnel of the Minnie Mine.

Lopez took Stefano's rifle, some shells, blankets, clothes and food and entered the Minnie Mine. Stefano told the mine's foreman, Tom Hoskins, what he knew and the posses gathered near the mouth of the Minnie.

Law officers, Apex mine officials and others in charge of the manhunt, had the openings to the mine sealed off and a huge fire was started in an attempt to smoke out Lopez.

After the fires burned out, a brief search was made inside the mine, but there was no sign of Lopez. It was decided to build the fire farther inside the mine, and hay and straw were carried inside to accomplish this.

On November 29, 1913, four men were moving bales of hay up the Andy incline in the mine when four shots were fired and two of the men, Douglas Hulsey and Joe Mandarich, were killed.

The guards were doubled and the fires started again. After burning for five days the fires were extinguished and the barricades removed. When the air cleared an extensive search of the mine was conducted but there was no trace of Lopez.

Lopez was never found. And the question has always remained: What happened?

The following year, with the Lopez story still fresh in everyone's mind, the town had another manhunt.

This one had its excitement, but it ended on a different note than the chase for Lopez.

At 3:30 P.M. on December 19, 1914, Bingham Canyon experienced its only bank robbery.

At that time, a 39-year-old man from Joplin, Mo., named Bert Heaton, entered the Bingham State Bank and stole $16,492.00 in gold and currency.

Working in the bank when Heaton entered that day were cashier Earl Randall, assistant cashier George Dobson and Henry Oddie, a 14-year-old office boy. Heaton drew a revolver and ordered the men to put their hands up. Then he forced Dobson and Oddie to lie on the floor where he tied their hands behind their backs. After binding Randall's hands behind his back, he forced the cashier to give him the combination to the safe, scooped out the money, locked the three employees in the vault and attempted to make his getaway.

He went down the canyon to the Bingham Coal and Lumber yard across the street from the Number 2 Fire Hall and crossed to the Star Livery to hire a rig.

But while Heaton was hurrying downtown, the men in the vault had freed themselves. Oddie had received a new pocketknife as a Christmas present. Dobson was able to take the knife from the boy's pocket and cut their bonds. Randall took a screwdriver, kept inside the vault for emergencies, and removed the plate from the locking device and opened the door.

Randall immediately got on the telephone and started to spread the alarm. One of the first persons he contacted was Isador Gauchet at the Bingham Coal and Lumber office. As Randall was describing the robber, Heaton walked past the office window. Gauchet hung up the phone and picked up a rifle. At the Star Livery, Rex Holden had been listening on the phone and when Heaton walked in he recognized him as the bank robber.

A stableboy was told to stall Heaton and he did until the robber became nervous and left. The stableboy saw him take refuge in an outhouse and led Holden and policeman Jim White to the building where Heaton was arrested.

Only 30 minutes elapsed from the time Heaton entered the bank until he was taken prisoner in the outhouse.

Two other robberies are worthy of mention.

In 1914, someone broke into Ed Zwicky's Highland Boy Store and in the process made enough noise to wake up a miner who lived in a cottage near the store and who is known only by his last name which was Allen.

Allen went to investigate the noise and was shot and killed. The murder was never solved.

And, two weeks later to the night, the Miner's Merc in Copperfield was robbed.

Ed Johnson was working in the Miner's Merc as the nightwatchman and recalls:

"I had a room in the store where I slept. We were not required to stay awake but just to stay in the building. I had a gun under my pillow and there was a lot of music and singing from a Greek coffeehouse across the street and I guess I fell asleep listening to the music.

"Someone broke the glass in the back door, rifled the three cash registers which had about $10 in each, took some watches, razors, a box of shorts and pocket knives, but didn't disturb the big safe in the office.

"The next morning I went to breakfast where a friend asked me if I had noticed the broken glass. I hurried back to the Merc, notified the manager, George Bowen, and the police were called.

"The police questioned me, but I hadn't heard a thing and couldn't help. Then, one of the fellows who worked in the office, J. Leo Jensen, asked about the gun and looked under my pillow. The gun was missing. The thief had apparently taken it, too, and I never lived it down while anyone was around who remembers what happened."

Bingham had many excellent police officers including Williams, Grant, Phil Culleton, Stanley Davies, Bunny Contratto, Ross Marriott, Boyd Nerdin, Al Paitsch, Alvin John Peterson and Elmer Pantalone. But perhaps the two most familiar lawmen were cousins Jack and Jim Householder who served as Salt Lake County Deputy Sheriffs for the Bingham area for many years and were active in many phases of life in the canyon.

One of Bingham's best known municipal judges was Ray Hamilton Kenner. Judge Kenner was born in Salt Lake City on November 5, 1872, and went to Bingham as a young man. There he engaged in leasing, prospecting and other mining development work and became involved in the town's civic and religious life. He served as judge from 1926 until his death in November, 1934. He had been re-elected as judge the Tuesday before his death.

Yes, from 1904, until the very end, Bingham Canyon was in its own hands and they were always capable hands.

And, although it took 34 years to happen, in 1938 the town of Bingham Canyon, Utah, became a third class city. The mayor that year was Edwin W. Johnson who had almost been born on the mountaintop.

FACTS AND FIGURES

The decade in which Bingham became a third class city reveals some interesting statistics on the town.

The following facts were listed in the 1941 Galena Days program:

Population—U.S. government census (1940): Bingham, 2,834; Copperton, 861; Highland Boy, 587; Lark, 515; Copperfield, 1,134; Total 5,931.

Elevation—6090 feet above sea level.

Schools—Bingham high and junior high school, Bingham Central school, Upper Bingham school, Highland Boy school, Copperton grade school, Lark grade school.

Churches—LDS churches, Holy Rosary Catholic church, Community Methodist church, Swedish Lutheran church.

Civic Organizations—Community Chest, Junior Chamber of Commerce, American Legion auxiliary, Women's Civic club, Bingham volunteer firemen companies No. 1 and No. 2, American Red Cross, Bingham Boy Scout council.

Modern sewer system.

Daily garbage collection—to all parts of the city.

Plentiful supply pure, cold mountain water.

Low tax rate—assessed valuation for $2,032,392; levy set at 15 mills.

Excellent playground facilities.

Superior fire protection.

Paved streets and sidewalks.

City health officer.

Four city police officers, two Salt Lake county deputy sheriffs.

1940 circulation in three branch libraries of Salt Lake county system—47,063.

An ideal four-season climate.

Excellent medical service—Bingham Canyon hospital and clinic and Utah Copper mines hospital.

Annual payroll figures, 1940—Utah Copper company (Bingham mine), $3,340,000; Combined payroll for Lark and Bingham operations United States Smelting, Mining and Refining company, $1,201,000; National Tunnel and Mines company, $310,046.68; Combined Metals Reduction company (Butterfield Canyon), $231,265.82; Ohio Copper Company of Utah, $70,852.06.

CHAPTER THREE

BINGHAM SONS AND DAUGHTERS

THE SMITH ROOMS in the Royal Apartments at the corner of Carr Fork were directly above the candy store and, usually, all kinds of delicious smells would tantalize 17-year-old Jack Smith when he sat at the kitchen table doing his homework. But this night Jack Smith was oblivious to any outside influence. He sat with his head bent over a sheet of paper and wrote furiously.

It was early in 1930, and Jack was a senior at Bingham High School which was located in the Bingham Central School building across from the Canyon Hall and Garage by Markham Gulch. This would be the last year the high school would hold its classes in the "Blue Prison." The next year it would be in the new building in Copperton, and the studentbody was conducting a contest to select a school song.

Jack Smith was a member of the school's baseball team, a powerfully-built athlete who played first base and was a long-ball hitter. He was also a fine singer and sang with groups from time to time, but had a dread of singing alone. He also liked to write poetry and was now intent on composing the words he hoped would become Bingham's school song.

At last he finished writing. Then to the tune of the "Sons of Burgundy," Jack sang his composition:

"Bingham sons and daughters
Like the mighty waters
Roll along to victory
Tides of Warriors greet us
With their teams to beat us
But we'll fight for victory.
Onward, onward team against the foe
Forward, forward our honored banners go.
All our foes will tremble
As our teams assemble,
On, on, on to victory.

Hear the echoes ringing
Hear the students singing
'Tis our song of victory,
Colors flying o'er us,
Blue and white before us,
Lead us on to victory.
Onward, onward team against the foe
Forward, forward the Bingham Miners go.
Bingham we are with you
And we're here to cheer you
Fight, fight, fight for victory."

When the contest was over and the winning song selected, an assembly was held in the third floor auditorium to introduce the song to the students. Principal H. R. Atkins announced that Jack Smith's entry had been selected and called him up to the stand. There he presented him with a check for $7.50 and said, "and now Jack will sing his song, 'Bingham Sons and Daughters.' "

The husky athlete blushed furiously, handed the check back and said, "Like heck, I will," and walked away.

"I hated the idea of singing solos. When I was in high school I sang in groups, but not alone. I just wouldn't do it," he explained his refusal to sing that historic afternoon.

"Bingham Sons and Daughters" is still the school song, but in 1964, a school hymn was written by Robert Knotts and Lowell Hicks. It is sung at all official functions and after each assembly. Its words are as follows:

"DREAMS OF BINGHAM HIGH"

"Day is ending night is blending, stars among the blue
Memories wander while we ponder school days fond
and true.
As the golden sun sets in the west—
We lay our dreams of Bingham High to rest.

We'll always remember the blue and the white
And faces so tender and dear—
We'll always remember the stars in the night
That shine on our campus so clear.
We'll always remember the laughs and the smiles
And the struggles, the sorrows and tears.
But though we may travel o'er many strange miles,
We'll always remember in May and September—
Bingham High and our happiest years."

Education always played an important role in Bingham Canyon. Prior to 1890, the children were apparently taught in private homes, but in the last decade of the 'eighties a school building was apparently in operation.

An item in the *Bingham Bulletin's* first issue on July 5, 1891, said:

"Upper Bingham has a fine school with an attendance of about 35. It is taught by Miss Ellen Rogers, who had charge of it last year. As the regular fund has been exhausted, the school will be continued this summer by private conscription. A new, larger building will be erected this season."

The new, larger school was a frame building at the corner of Main and Markham Gulch. It was the start of the Canyon Hall.

Canyon Hall was built over Markham Creek and there were planks placed across the creek to the playground below the Red Wing Mill. Ed Johnson recalls a day when one of the girls lost a ring while crossing the plank and the boys spent hours in the creek trying to find the ring. He also recalls the long lines that formed in front of the outdoor toilet at recess and the day when, inevitably, a boy somehow fell into the deep hole in the privy.

"It was very deep and we couldn't reach him. He was yelling for help and it was a real mess. Finally, we got two men to come from the Red Wing Mill. They brought a long rope, dropped one end to him and pulled him out," Johnson said.

The first high school was built north of the Canyon Hall on the west side of the canyon and the earliest high school graduating class seems to be 1912.

Sometime in 1906, the old Central School was built just below the high school. It was stone and brick topped by a cupola with a bell. The Jordan School District consolidated in 1905, and Bingham was now part of the district.

In 1918, the gymnasium building was completed just below the Central school so there were three school buildings in a row on the lot there.

The first, second and third grades used the Central school, the fourth, fifth and sixth grades were located on the top floor of the gymnasium and the higher grades used the high school.

In 1918 the first year book published by Bingham High School students was produced and was called "Metal." The foreword said: "To us, this first volume of the *Metal* shall preserve the memory of many happy hours spent in pleasant companionship. In future years we shall turn from discouragement and disappointment to this picture of courage and confidence and stimulated by it, pledge again faith in ourselves and in our fellowmen.

"To the public this volume shall reveal our earnest and honest efforts to prepare ourselves to hold places of trust and confidence in our community. Should the *Metal* accomplish these ends it will have fulfilled our hopes for it."

—THE EDITORS

The first *Metal* was dedicated to Inez Todd King, a member of the faculty. I. W. Nielsen was principal and the teachers were: P. S. Marthakis, science and mathematics; Erna P. Spitzenberger, history; E. Rose and C. McDonough, home economics; Inez Todd King, English and dramatics; Mildred A. Mattson, commercc; in addition to his duties as principal, Nielsen taught language; Albert J. Southwick, music; Josephine Sherman, junior high; H. P. Christensen, physical education; Roy Gardner, manual arts; Vivian Gardner, junior high, and Nan Pierson, junior high.

This was the year of America's participation in World War I, and high school members in the service were listed as: Robert Wilson, Vernon Guymon, George Marshall, Thomas Wilson, Elmer Eden, Clyde Tibbles, Alphonso Terry and William McDonough.

Clyde W. Countryman was senior class president and there were only five members of the senior class that year. The others were Clesta Paul, Margaret Tennant, Mark L. James and Thomas Jenkins.

When the Class of 1918 entered the high school in 1914 there were 36 students in the class. By the time it started its junior year the class had dwindled to seven and only five graduated. Noting this fact, the class members said, "We are only five, but we mean to show our loving parents and our teachers that the hours of toil and worry they have spent, trying to instill in us the principles of right living have not been wasted. . . . We leave the school our love and gratitude. We thank our parents for their sacrifice in sending us to school and some day, you may be sure that we are going to show the world that Bingham is a good place to raise and educate children."

The school song at that time had no other title and was sung to the tune of "Dixie."

The words were:

"My heart's in love with our good old Bingham
Copper mountains, and girls in gingham.
So I pray
Let me stay
In Bingham town.

Chorus

Then let me stay in Bingham, Hooray, Hooray.
With Bingham's band I'll take my stand, to live and die in Bingham.
Away, I'll pray, to stay out west in Bingham.

Second Verse

Her sons will prove they are the bravest heroes
When they fight the Prussian Neroes.
When they fight, then good night to Kaiser Bill
When they have "hoched" and "hoched" "Der Kaiser", Poor old Bill will be much wiser.
Look out Bill, Bitter Pill, Our Bingham boys.
Oh! Bingham girls they are queens in betting
In their heads no room for letting
They're so sweet, no girls beat Our Bingham girls.

And so we're loyal to the core, to school, to team
and things galore.
You'll be fleet, if you beat, our Bingham High."

The junior class that year would be the last class to graduate in the decade. Its members were: Alfred Anderson, Annie Masters, Lillian Chiara, Gladys Jones, Dorothy Kappele, Esther Ball, Lola Royce, Fae Patten, Mary Wade, Ada Clays, Elmer Whiteley, Dewey Miller and Lester Schoettlin.

The sophomores would be the first class to graduate in the new decade and its members included: Lyon Barnard, Pearl Adderley, Bert Shaw, Victor Ashworth, Gertrude Liljeroth, Doris Stapleton, LaVern Jones, Severn Granquist, Harold Anderson, Hadee Adams, Byron Green, Margaret Gaythwaite, Hugh Glenn, Ethel Nowers, Stephen Wright, Clara Christensen, Cerald Erickson, Chris Plates, Miles Gaythwaite, Bert Terry, Vivian Drew, Richard Guyman.

Members of the freshmen class were: Choloe Dean, Ruth Clays, Thelma Croy, May Farrel, Marie Nelson, Ova Countryman, Melba Jennings, Hilda Tregaskis, Vernon Erickson, George Marthakis, George Knudsen, John Gregory, Pete Musilli, Ellen Siddoway, Lester Randall, Mary Culleton, Fred Hoskings, Kaythleen Nowers, Rose Geffen, Leonard Hyland, May Nix, Pete Pitchos, Archie James, Arnold Beales, Irvan Stillman, Kenneth Russell, Fred Turner and William Oddie.

Mona G. Heaston, who was a member of the school's first graduating class in 1912, added some alumni notes which told what former students were doing six years after the first class left the school:

Clifford A. Mayer, class of 1912, with National Geographic Society in Washington, D.C.

Agnes McDonald, '12, now Mrs. Daniel F. Sullivan, teaching at Garfield.

Elvira Christensen, '12, in Long Beach, Calif.

David I. Geffen, '12, in U.S. Navy.

Mona G. Heaston, '12, in Bingham Post office.

Leonard Porter, '13, in West Coast shipyards.

Della Jenkins, now Mrs. Joe Neilson, home on Boston Con hill.

Charles W. Adderley, '16, with his father in Bingham Merc.

Henry Oddie, assistant cashier at Citizens' State Bank.

M. Louise Dudley, '17, now wife of Lt. Victor Eckman in Kansas.

Joe Mayer, '17, at University of Utah.

Maisie D. Adderley, '17, working at Bingham Merc.

Agnes James, '17, helps in her father's stationery store.

Michael Boccalero, '17, at University of Utah.

John Culleton, '17, at Bingham Merc.

Robert Wilson, '17, in army.

Vernon Guyman, '17, first Bingham boy to reach France, with marines.

Ida Sagner, '17, attending girl's school in San Francisco.

Dottie Stringham, '17, taking post-graduate course at high school.

John Strickley, '17, in auto service station in Salt Lake City.

Roy Knowles, '17, at Denver & Rio Grande yards in Welby.

Rennie Nichols, '17, at U.P.&L.

Lucille Dixon, '17, in Ogden.

Eva Burke, '17, with her mother on Boston Con hill.

Nellie Klopenstine, '13, now Mrs. M. A. Cotter.

Ernest Dean, '13, joined aviation section of signal corps.

Cecelia Geffen, '14, popular grade teacher in Bingham school.

Berton M. Fitzgerald, '14, Lt. balloon observation corps.

Della O. Coakley, '15, at Bingham post office.

Julius Hill, '15, in mercantile business.

Daisy M. Adderley, '16, at Bingham post office.

Florence Grant, '16, chief operator Bingham telephone office.

As mentioned, the first issue of the *Metal* was dedicated to Inez Todd King who came to Bingham Canyon to teach in 1913 and the first class she followed through high school was the class of 1917. In the *Metal* the young teacher wrote some words that could apply to every class that went through Bingham High School.

She said:

"I remember well the day I first looked into the faces of the Freshmen, the senior class of 1917. Restless, fun-loving, mischievous, with bobbing heads, laughing eyes, and feet that somehow always found their way into the aisle for some unfortunate fellow classmate to stumble over, the class presented a real problem. Mr. Alston, who was principal at that time, explained to me the first day, that the freshman class had been marked from the fifth grade up as 'hustlers.' I found this to be true, although they did not always "hustle" in the right direction, for they were quite as apt to hustle away from work, as toward it. It may also be said they were always open to conviction and ready to yield to guidance. Their restless energy directed into lines of usefulness has made them known as the class who did things. . . .

"This vivacious class little knew what a large part they played in the education of a tenderfoot, fresh from an eastern city. With failing heart I followed them upon some of their daring mountain climbs, awed by the mystery of the dark mountain scenery, as the sun went down behind the mighty peaks and the sound of the blasting from the great mines reverberated from peak to peak filling the air above, the ground below, with whispering echoes of wild, undreamed of music, that added to the majesty of the night. I knew that God had given Bingham children the opportunity for an education broader than that offered by any college—the chance to know God, Himself, through the teaching of nature. . . .

"How could man be mean or small in the shadow of these mighty mountains, in a place where such big things are being accomplished, as in Bingham Canyon?

"A year ago, some of the boys of the class of 1917 responded to the nation's call for men. We walked with them to the depot to tell them "God speed." As I looked into their faces my thoughts went back over the time I had known them. It did not seem possible that these calm, quiet men were the boys who but yesterday had been eagerly looking for some new prank with which to astonish their fellows. They stood there, shoulders squared, heads up, eyes bright, the spirit of the camp, made flesh and blood.

"Beside them stood the boys and girls who had been playmates and companions in the childhood which had vanished forever. In their faces was no sign of hysteria. Each wore a smile—a little tremulous, perhaps—but nevertheless courageous. The Class of 1917 sent its forces away with a smile, and so, man and woman, it won its first great battle of life—the fight for self-control and self-forgetfulness.

"God bless them all. They are splendid representatives of the camp, active, fearless and loyal, endowed with the spirit of youth, and the self-control which the majesty of the mountains which surround Bingham, gives to all the people who lift their eyes to the white peaks."

In 1925, the new Bingham Central opened its doors and the upper grades moved in. Bingham Central was a big, brick building located just north of the Red Wing Mill and soon was nicknamed, "The Old Blue Prison" by students.

With the upper grades now housed in the new school, students in the first six grades moved into the old high school and the old Central school was torn down.

In the fall of 1931, the new high school opened at Copperton with the junior and high school housed there. The grade school moved into Bingham Central and the old high school was abandoned and later razed.

The gym building alone remained of the three old school buildings on that lot. The swimming pool crumbled and the building deteriorated for awhile. Then, in 1935, the American Legion took it over as the Civic Center.

There was another school early residents remember. The Methodist Church maintained deaconess schools there and at least a kindergarten was held in the Community Church just below the Bingham Central.

Everard Cowdell, who later owned the Bingham Radio store uptown, remembers first going to school in the Community Church, and of cutting wood for the pot-bellied stove that heated the large room where classes were held. And many canyon residents who entered the first grade in the old Central school, first attended kindergarten in the Community Church.

Copperfield School consisted of six classrooms, a library, principal's office and gymnasium.

Highland Boy's eight-room school was destroyed by fire in 1932, but a new school was built there in 1936.

The high school always served all the regions of Bingham and when it was established at Copperton, students were transported there by bus from Copperfield, Highland Boy, Bingham and Lark.

In the early days, the headmaster of the school was over all the classes. One of the first teachers was C. L. Countryman, who arrived on the scene in 1897, and he was followed by Judge E. E. Dudley.

In 1911, Howard Alston was principal, followed by Art Willard, L. W. Nielson and Howard Atkin. When the high school moved to Copperton it was necessary to have separate principals in the high school and grade schools. Tommy McMullin became principal of the high school. Other high school principals following Mr. McMullin were H. W. Jorgenson, Joel P. Jensen, Don J. Parr, Richard A. Bateman and Glen L. Beere.

On March 28, 1946, a banquet was held in the high school honoring McMullin for his 25 years service to the school and community. Speakers included Governor Herbert B. Maw and Utah State Coach E. L. "Dick" Romney. Representatives of each high school class starting in 1922 gave a short talk paying tribute to "Tommy."

Class representatives were:

Class of 1922, Ruth Granquist; 1923, Lawrence E. Stillman; 1924, Dora Thomas; 1925, Avery Masters; 1926, Frances Ball Morley; 1927, Eskel Johnson; 1928, Willard and Norma Nichols; 1929, Rennold Contratto; 1930, Harley English; 1931, Chris Praggastis; 1932, Billy Johnson; 1933, Clair Johnson; 1934, Virginia Harris; 1935, John Bolic; 1936, Ellen Carl; 1937, Blaine Wells; 1938, Hosmer Peterson; 1939, Mary Serassio; 1940, Marian Jimas; 1941, Stanley and Delana Long; 1942, Peter Dimas; 1943, George Furgis; 1944, Mary Drossos; 1945, Don Prigmore and 1946, Irene Curry and Kenneth Hall.

Most of the teachers and principals in Bingham's history are remembered for their educational contributions. An exception was Art Willard who was involved in a tragic eternal triangle.

Willard and his wife had a boarder, a young student named Cecil Holmes who was an excellent basketball player. Willard became convinced his wife and Holmes were having an affair and the two men became involved in a fight. Later, while Holmes was getting a haircut in a barbershop north of the Society Hall, Willard walked in with a gun and shot and killed his former protege.

Willard was acquitted of a murder charge and left the town.

The shooting shocked the town which indicates Bingham was not the rough town it was reputed to be or what would one more shooting mean?

When Bingham's sons and daughters moved from the old school to Bingham Central it was a move that was only across the street and up the road a few feet, but it was like moving from the city to the country as far as space was concerned.

The old high school had a door that opened right onto the street. There was no space at all. The old Central school was set only slightly back and its playground was the side of the mountain that loomed only a few small feet from the back doors and windows.

But Bingham Central had a playground in front with swings, slides, rings, tricky bars. The now unused mill still stood there, but this, too, was a playground, although a potentially dangerous one.

There was a principal's office on the first floor just across the hall and up the small flight of stairs from the front door. There were 12 classrooms, a library and an auditorium. It was modern and new and the young students thought of it as being exceptionally beautiful. It had room for more than 300 students and it was more crowded than usual because students from Highland Boy attended school there until their new building became ready in 1936.

But, if the elementary students were enchanted, not all their teachers shared their opinion.

One young lady, there on her first teaching assignment, was teaching her fourth grade pupils about the United States and one day read to them about Pittsburgh, Pennsylvania, and its reputation as the smoky city. She put the book down on her desk, stood in front of the class and said angrily:

"Whoever wrote that story about Pittsburgh never saw Bingham Canyon. If he had come here he would have called this town the smoky city."

She paused and looked at her pupils, many of them with dirty hands and faces from playing in the dirt and almost all of them in clothing that had been handed down from older brothers or sisters and was worn and patched and some of it even dirty.

"This is the most filthy place in the world. It is smoky and dirty. The houses are dirty. Everything in the town is dirty. You can't touch anything without getting your hands or clothes filthy. This is the dirtiest town in the world, not Pittsburgh."

The students sat silent under the outburst, but at least one, looked out the window and thought, "That isn't true. It might be dirty, but it isn't that bad. It isn't the dirtiest in the whole world."

There is no doubt that Bingham Canyon was dirty. It was a town almost inside a mine. When the students at Bingham Central ate their noon lunch, they took their small lunch pails, paper bags or tin pails and hurried to a favorite eating place on the mountain. They sat on the ground or on an old railroad tie or a cribbing.

After eating they played on the playground if a swing or bar or slide was available. If not, they ran up and down the hills and investigated the old mill.

There was no clean, green lawn available. There was dirt and rocks and because they came from houses that were also built on the dirt and rocks, they didn't notice.

And when an outsider told them their town was dirty, they refused to believe it.

But teachers who hated the town and its noise and smoke and dirt and the children that went with it, were few. Many were dedicated and sincere and were there to teach. One of these, a Miss Butterfield, taught reading, writing and arithmetic to hundreds of Bingham students.

Every student undoubtedly remembers those who were so understanding.

Not long after the elementary classes moved into Bingham Central, two members of the faculty were Binghamites. They were Beatrice Spendlove and Virginia Ivie.

Miss Spendlove was a well-loved young teacher who wrote a history of Bingham Canyon as her master's thesis at the University of Utah. Later she married and as Beatrice Spendlove Bates, she returned to teach at Bingham High School where she is teaching at this time.

Miss Ivie brought a love of the legitimate theater to her classrooms. She encouraged her young pupils to take part in school plays and she left her love of make believe with many of those boys and girls whose reality was a shanty on a dirt road.

Having the high school at Copperton also added a new dimension to the lives of Bingham students.

The high school consisted of the administration and classroom building, a gymnasium, auditorium, garage and shops all on a well-landscaped campus. A stadium was built in a natural setting in the foothills behind the school.

The faculty at Bingham High School underwent some changes each year, but many former Miners have their own memories of such teachers as:

Charles Crawford, who was also assistant principal of the junior high; Coordinator David Wootten; Coach Allsop; Coach Santistevan; Bernice Anderson, secretarial science; Vernon Baer, English; Robert Bailey, mathematics; Byron Birch, chemistry and science; Robert Payne, English; Clement Crapo, music; Myrth Harvey, English; Joel Jensen, music and principal; Paul Kuhni, art; Laura Marshall, English; Victoria Peternel, commercial courses; Odell Peterson, history, mathematics, tennis coach; Clarence Pollard, social science; Ellen Sampson, English; James Seal, industrial arts; Mildred Seal, library; Marie Singleton, girls physical education; Virginia Harris McDonald, girls physical education; Reho Thorum, social science; Verna Walker, home economics; James Woodhouse, mechanics and transportation and Howard Hauscknecht, mechanics and transportation.

Among the office secretaries who served long and faithfully were Margaret Ireland and Tillie (Mrs. Dick) Steele. Helen Stillman Peterson and Mary Linn Gaythwaite Sanderson are still there.

Oley Jensen and Otto Carpenter were in charge of maintenance. Bus drivers included Joe Timothy and Verl Peterson.

Among the former Bingham High School students who returned to teach at their alma mater were, June Culbertson, Virginia Harris McDonald, Beatrice Spendlove Bates, Cal Crump, Tom Pazell, George Sluga, Ted Sandstrom and Linda Long Sandstrom.

One of the veteran teachers in the Bingham Central and Copperton elementary schools was Maude Stillman who came to Bingham as a senior, married Lawrence "Tuffy" Stillman and after his death in 1951, went back to teaching school.

In 1975, the Jordan School District will open a new high school in South Jordan and it will replace the high school at Copperton. But there will always be a Bingham High School. When the decision to build the new school at South Jordan was announced, the students at Copperton voted to retain the name of Bingham High School.

CHAPTER FOUR

BIG, SMALL, OLD AND NEW

THEY CALLED IT the "Big Store" and they did well to call it that. For most of its career it sat on the corner of Carr Fork and Main and it seemed to cover a city block. The street level floor was the grocery and meat department. The Main Street entrance took customers into the clothing departments. The Carr Fork entrance was into the hardware section. The Main Street and Carr Fork entrances were both reached by climbing up a flight of wooden stairs and on the Main Street side there was a porch running the length of the store.

The porch and the steps on both sides were important to the community. On the main Street side band concerts were held there. Patriotic and campaign speeches were delivered there. In World War II, Abbott and Costello put on their act there to sell war bonds. Miners going off shift and waiting for rides to the valley below, waited on the steps, especially on the Carr Fork side.

It was the Bingham Mercantile Company Store and, sometime or other, some way or other, it touched the lives of all Bingham Canyon residents.

It was not the first store in Bingham Canyon, but it had a direct link with the first store. Its founder and president was Charles E. Adderley, a distinguished-looking businessman from New York who arrived on the scene when Bingham was a mining camp and stayed to become one of the steadying hands that turned the camp into a town and the town into a solid, secure community.

The first store in the canyon was a small grocery store owned by a Mr. Lashbrook and located about two-and-a-half miles from where Bingham Canyon's town would be located.

John Strickley opened the first grocery store in the city limits and his establishment bore the impressive title of "John Strickley and son General Merchandise and Miner's Outfitting Store."

Charles E. Adderley served an apprenticeship in both Lashbrook's and Strickland's stores before going into business for himself in the canyon town.

In 1906, Adderley opened the doors of the first Bingham Mercantile Store. It was a small building and was located in the area where the Social Hall stood during most of the town's history. From there Adderley moved across the street into a building that later served as a warehouse for the "Big Store." It was around 1906, when he moved the Bingham Merc to its final location, incorporated and thus launched one of the town's most important and successful enterprises.

The Adderley's had four children, all of whom were important citizens of Bingham. They were: Charles W. (Chick) Adderley, Daisy (Mrs. Kenneth Bogart), Maisie (Mrs. Rex Tripp) and Pearl (Mrs. Ren Nichols).

Rex Tripp Sr. was one of the store's top officers. Employees in the store over the years included Ed W. Johnson, Jay and Harry Mitchell, Mrs. Zion, Cora Hocking, Ross Hocking, John Hocking, Connie Mackazuka, Daisy Bogart, Lillian Rasmussen, Ann Pechina (Slattery), Pearl Walcott, Maude Hocking, Ester Clays, Jennie Tome, Ray Kopesec, Dee Rasmussen, Lois Taylor, Aaron Beard, Bert Hocking,

Otto Lee, Elwood Johnson, Eva West, Myrtle Peterson, Leonard Miller, and among the delivery truck drivers were Leonard Carlson, Steve Smilanich and Eddie Jacobsen.

In 1873, a man who was to have a tremendous influence on many of the miners made his appearance as a businessman in Bingham Canyon.

That year Steven Hays, in partnership with Patrick Phelan, opened a general mining supplies store in the camp. By 1901, Hays had bought out his partner and was advertising his business as, "S. Hays, successor to Phelan and Hays, general mining supplies established in 1873."

Steve Hays was more than a storekeeper. He was banker to half of the people in Bingham Canyon for many years. He made it a practice to grubstake miners going 50-50 on any strikes.

Isadore Morris is another of the early businessmen. From 1874 to 1884, Morris ran a general store and one corner of his building was set off as a post office.

In 1891, a young printer from Missouri, Ed K. Watts, established the *Bingham Bulletin* and in his first edition dated July 5, 1891, editor Watts said the paper was started with "the brightest hopes and most sanguine expectations for the future of Bingham and her citizens."

Watts referred to Bingham Canyon as the "Old Reliable" and said it was with confidence that he started his newspaper in "one of the oldest, richest and best mining camps in the West."

From its first issue, the *Bingham Bulletin* never wanted for advertisers. In those days it was called the *Bingham Press Bulletin.*

In the issue of July 5, 1891, the paper carried the following advertisements:

"B. B. Quinn, notary public and conveyancer; Brown, Cushing and Hadley, Do-Drop-In Saloon; M. A. Vivian, general merchandise; A. Klopenstine, Griffin Hotel; Bourgard and Kilburn, Mountain Belle Saloon; J. B. Steven, premium boot and shoemaker, rubber goods; John Strickley and Son, general merchandise and miner's outfitting store; F. J. Flynn, physician and surgeon; Henry Marriott, practical blacksmithig; Dr. A. L. Castleman, physician and surgeon; Humphrey and Balderstrom, assaying and surveying; Cushing, Hadley and Kay, dealers in everything; W. E. Jones, Beer Depot; P. Tavey, druggist and stationer, wines and liquors; S. Hays, successor to Phelan and Hays, general mining supplies, established 1873; the Happy Hour Dental Company with two ladies' and two gentlemen's attendants."

It also carried a list of cards announcing the availability of numerous attorneys in Salt Lake City.

The *Bingham Bulletin* would survive its early advertisers. When the paper celebrated its 50th anniversary on June 5, 1941, it could point proudly to being the "oldest business institution in Bingham Canyon."

In 1961, the *Bingham Bulletin* moved its shop to West Jordan and there was no newspaper on Bingham Canyon's main street for the first time in 70 years.

Among the editors of the *Bingham Bulletin* following Watts, were Ira Masters, Phil Goldwater, J. R. Jarvis, Howard C. Barrows, Leland G. Burress and John Adamek. Adamek joined the paper's staff in January, 1936, became editor in 1945, and was the last owner and publisher of the paper.

The *Bingham News* was published for a short while in the late 1920's and early '30's. It was started by Herbert Gust, another of the town's most familiar figures. It was sold to George Reynolds and eventually went out of business. Like the *Bulletin,* it was also located in the main business district in the upper part of the town.

A local tailor, Otto Kappel, published a small paper for awhile.

Except for the times when a fire or other natural disaster ravaged sections of the town forcing the area to be rebuilt, most of the business buildings in Bingham Canyon remained the same over the years although the occupants and type of endeavor changed from time to time.

It was a town of small businesses and these were run by men and women who dealt with their customers on a personal basis.

Drug stores were places to fill prescriptions, purchase personal items and to have an ice cream soda or banana split. At George Evans' Bingham Drug it was popular to try the odd and even punchboard where an even number paid off with a dime's worth of candy while an odd just meant you had lost your nickel. Other drug stores included the Webb Drug and the Union Drug which was originally in Copperfield and owned by Jim Jimas, but later opened in Bingham Canyon under his son, Bob Jimas. The town's first druggist was Peter Tavey.

In the early years, the Bourgard Butcher Shop was an impressive meat market and was located on the space where the Post Office was built in 1933. Bourgard's was destroyed by the fire of 1924, and the Bingham Meat became the town's leading butcher shop.

Bingham Meat was started by Ben Dietrich and was managed by his widow for awhile after his death. Then Bill Harris and the Robison brothers bought it. In the late 1950's, Mr. Harris ran the shop alone and he was connected with it until it went out of business.

The Bingham Meat ran a delivery service and its truck was a familiar sight in all parts of the community.

But meat delivery had long roots in the canyon town.

When Ed Johnson was a small boy enrolled in the Canyon Hall school, he was introduced to the meat cutting and delivery business by working for the "Valley Butcher," David Bills.

Bills operated out of Riverton. He would load his wagon with meat and drive the team and wagon across the flats to the canyon.

"He would visit Bingham Canyon on Wednesday and Saturday. I would listen for the bell he rang as soon as he came into town to announce the meat wagon was here, and I would hurry to meet him. I drove the team and helped the customers and learned to cut meat," Johnson recalled.

"When we pulled into an area of homes, I would ring the bell and the housewives would come out to the wagon with platters. The women would select the meat they wanted, Mr. Bills would cut it and pile it on their big platters. If a customer wanted more meat than her platter would hold, I carried the extra meat to her house and I helped by carrying eggs and butter for the women," he added.

Other peddlers visited Bingham both in the early days when they were practically the only source of fresh produce and meat and through the 1930's and '40's.

Jake Greenwood was the first big peddler to visit Bingham Canyon regularly. He was from American Fork and he catered to the boarding houses starting at the city limits and delivering all the way up the main canyon to the U.S. Commercial Boarding House in the Copperfield region.

Greenwood's caravan of five or six wagons, all loaded with produce, would headquarter at Chandler's Livery Stable where the Princess Theater stood later. There Greenwood's assistants slept in the hayloft or in one of the six or seven wooden shacks. Bingham boys would be hired for 25 cents a day to help with soliciting and deliveries. Greenwood was a big man, with a big stomach and he did a big business in Bingham.

The canyon's residents knew many peddlers. Some of these they called "sunshine peddlers" which meant they only came when the weather was good. Others came on regular days, rain or shine, winter or summer.

One peddler used to specialize in cabbages and his customers were mostly in Highland Boy where they bought the cabbages and made huge amounts of sauerkraut.

The Highland Boy region was also a good market for grape peddlers. The grapes were used to manufacture homemade wine and carloads of grapes used to pour into the region every fall.

Many peddlers were of Greek descent and some of them started their own stores in the canyon. Among these was Charley Dimas, who bought the store where he opened his Bingham Grocery Number 1 from another Greek pioneer of the town, John Speros, during World War I.

Charley operated the store below Hegland Alley in the Freeman-Dixon-Railroad Avenue area for more than 40 years. The Dimas' had three boys, Peter, Theodore and George, and two daughters, Katherine and Wilma.

Pete managed the store with his father almost from the time he was old enough to work behind the counter. Theodore was killed in the Philippines during World War II. George graduated from college, coached and taught in the Salt Lake area for a few years and then became the Director of the Foundation of Alcoholism for Oregon. Katherine has been a long-time employee in the Salt Lake Chamber of Commerce. But Pete stayed at the store in Bingham Canyon, operating it until there were not enough people left in the town to stay open. He and his family remained there with Pete serving as mayor from 1962, until the town was disincorporated on November 22, 1971.

Possibly because of the peddler influence, most of the grocery and meat market owners in the canyon offered free delivery service. This ranged all the way from the delivery trucks of the Bingham Merc and Bingham Meat to young Chris Apostol of Christ's Groceries and Meat Market in Frogtown, carrying a bag of groceries to Railroad Avenue and climbing the steps up the mountainside to Flora Amicone's home there.

The merchants of the canyon were generous with credit, especially during the depression years, and this enabled many of the miners and their families to make it over the hard times.

And for this reason, too, the merchants meant a great deal to life in the town.

Sometimes the bookkeeping was ultra-simplified. In the early days there was a Japanese boarding house in Carr Fork. One of the owners of a store there carried charge accounts on his books under the following headings:

"Jap No. 1, Jap No. 2, Jap No. 3," etc.

Copperfield and Highland Boy had their fine merchants and stores including the Miner's Mercantile Company, Landaris Mercantile and The Independent in Copperfield; The Highland Boy Mercantile Company, Johnson's Market, Canyon Merc, Gebhart's, and Nick Bolic's Slavonian Store in Highland Boy.

Among the Bingham stores were Chipian's Food Store, Tom Praggastis' store, Frank Shafter's store, Lott's, Dowd's Cash Grocery, Well's Grocery, Vienna Grocery, Muller's Grocery, Centre Market, Joe Schussel's Michigan Grocery, the Vietta Grocery, and Safeways.

One of the nation's first J. C. Penney stores was opened in the canyon and the founder of that chain lived in the town for awhile when he was getting started. Bill Grant, whose father figured in Bingham's most notorious manhunt as a sheriff, managed the Penney's store for years.

At one time it was known as The Golden Rule Store and Mr. Penney offered Bingham cleaning store owner Carl Meyers a chance to go into business with him as a partner in the Golden Rule chain.

Another of the best known stores in the town was the M. L. James Variety Store across from the Princess Theater. Mr. James was a postmaster in the town as was his son, Earl, and he was an astute businessman. It was he who sold the first radio in the town and he had a stock of radios, phonographs and records.

The Bingham Radio, owned by Everard Cowdell and Hugo Dellagnola before Dellagnola became the sole owner, made a trade for the first radio in town.

Cowdell traded Harvey Wolfe a radio for a Model T Ford.

There was a cigar manufacturing business in the canyon early in the 1900's. Big burlap sacks of tobacco leaves were delivered by Wells Fargo in containers of heavy straw. Boys were hired to smooth out the leaves which were rolled into bundles when they were delivered.

There was a penny arcade, a shooting gallery, roller skating rinks (the best known was in the Canyon Hall above Spud Morley's Canyon Garage at Markham and Main), four breweries, a bottling works and several mortuaries.

One of the mortuaries that went out of business by popular demand had the habit of using an available corpse as a dummy hand in a nightly game of sluff played by the owner and his friends. When the word got around, the establishment went out of business.

For a short time in the late 1920's, there was a miniature golf course where the post office was built.

There were several Chinese cafes and laundries. Frank Carr ran the Sturm Cafe, John Feraco had the Italian-French Bar and Cafe, and George Wells was a popular cafe owner.

Harry Noble's Vienna Cafe was a class establishment. Located between the Copper King and Bingham Livery it was a landmark with its glass fish tank in the window. It used linen napkins and tablecloths. A stairway led to an upstairs dining room and many Bingham residents were first introduced to finger bowls in the Vienna Cafe.

Barbering was not always the most profitable business in town because many of the fathers insisted on cutting their sons' hair, especially during the depression.

But there was enough business to keep several shops and many fine barbers busy cutting and talking.

Bruce and Golden Ivie ran a shop in the basement of the Bingham Merc. Jack Dean had a shop at 284 Main. When Dean left town to move to Salt Lake City, Bruce Ivie took over his shop. Bert Thaxton had a shop in the Copper King building and then in the Princess Theater building. "Funny" Bennett joined Thaxton as a partner when he moved into the theater site and Lew Collins was another barber in the shop.

Bill Goris ran a big shop in Carr Fork called the Utah Barber Shop. One of his barbers was Tony Xanthos who later operated the Big 4. George Klonizos ran a shop at 19 Carr Fork.

Jim Spanos had a shop for years in the building that housed the Furgis Apartments and Christ's Grocery and Meat in Frogtown. From there Spanos moved uptown to 151 Main and was one of the last barbers running a shop in the town.

The other barber who was still working there in the 1960's, was Andy Savich who had a shop at 479 Main in the Woodring Building. Savich had a shop in Highland Boy for years before transferring to Bingham.

It was December, 1918, and World War I was over and America was in a dizzy state of post-war speculation in mining stocks. At this time there were two banks in Bingham Canyon. One, the Bingham State Bank, was the first one to receive a charter and had opened its doors to the public on October 13, 1903, a year before the town incorporated. The other was the Bingham State Bank formed around 1910.

The Bingham State Bank was located in the town's first brick building adjoining the Steve Hays store. The Citizen's State Bank was in the Woodring Building.

They were to be involved in a dramatic experience on December 9, 1918. The Citizen's State Bank would fail and this failure would cause a run on the Bingham State Bank that could have been disastrous.

When it was organized the Citizen's State Bank's president was Rodney Badger and directors included, Dr. F. E. Straup and Jerome Bourgard, two of the town's most respected men. Cashier was Q. B. Kelly. Kelly was also the town's mayor at the time the bank failed.

There has been no official explanation of what happened to the bank's assets but when it didn't open that winter day in 1918, many of its depositors panicked and became angry. This caused fear among those with money in the Bingham State Bank and they rushed there to withdraw their savings fearing that it, too, might be in danger of folding.

Naturally, this caught the bank unprepared. Cashier Earl Randall tried to cope with the situation. While he was calming customers, an emergency meeting was held by the directors and officers. A courier was rushed by automobile to Salt Lake City where he turned all of the bank's available assets into cash and sped back to Bingham Canyon with the currency stacked in a large basket.

The basket was emptied in dramatic fashion, the currency placed on top of a table in plain view of the depositors lined up to withdraw their money. The sight of the cash calmed the fears of some customers who left without withdrawing their savings. But most of the customers stayed on, received their cash and left.

It was a touchy time, but the bank had enough money to pay off its obligations and remain in business. It was a close call, but quick thinking and quick action saved the day.

There were a couple of sorry aftermaths to the failure of the Citizen's State Bank. Cashier Kelly, never accused of wrong doing, resigned as mayor and with his family moved out of town. And a rift developed between the post office and the remaining bank, the Bingham State Bank.

After the people had taken their money out of the bank, many of them went straight to the post office and deposited it in postal savings. Bank officials asked the postmaster to deposit the money in the bank as usual that evening, probably to show the town's citizens that the government had faith in the bank. But the postmaster refused and a wound was opened that took a long time to heal.

The failure of the Citizen's State Bank and the resulting run on its competitor, were the most dramatic events in the history of banking in Bingham Canyon.

Banking was an informal business in the early days in Bingham Canyon. Steve Hays furnished grubstakes for many miners and served as an unofficial banker through the offices of his store and could be regarded as the town's first banker.

On October 13, 1903, a charter was issued to the Bingham State Bank making it the first one in the canyon.

On May 2, 1929, the bank changed its name to the First Security Bank of Bingham. Stockholders who voted for the change in name are listed as L. S. Cates, F. D. Moffat, C. E. Adderley, J. D. Shilling, Charles T. S. Parsons and First Security Corporation of Ogden. Cates was listed as president and Parsons as secretary.

In the 1920's, the First National Bank of Bingham was established with George E. Chandler, president, and Eugene Chandler, cashier. The bank was located in Chandler's new Princess Theater building but it didn't last long.

On April 4, 1930, the First Security Bank of Bingham took over assets and liabilities of the First National Bank of Bingham which went into voluntary liquidation and merged with Bingham's First Security. The Chandlers signed the agreement for the First National Bank while C. E. Adderley, president, and Parsons, secretary, signed for First Security.

Not long after the Citizen's State Bank failed, another bank was formed. This one, named the Central Bank, was also located in the Woodring Building and the cashier was Reuben T. Dahlquist who later became a Salt Lake County commissioner.

It was natural for the citizens of the town to turn to the post office after the run on the bank. The post office was a friend. Many of the residents of Bingham Canyon came from Europe or the Far East. The post office brought them letters from the homeland and delivered letters to friends and relatives who had stayed behind. The post office employees in Bingham Canyon had a long record of outstanding service from the camp days to the town's end and this record was well established by the end of World War I.

The first post office operated in the camp in 1870, and Thomas Matthews was postmaster. Joseph Goddard handled the mail the same year. Fred J. Kiesel was postmaster in

1872, and Isador Morris had the post office in a corner of his store from 1874 to 1884.

It was moved to the Phelan and Hays store in 1885, with Patrick Phelan as postmaster. Bernard Quinn took over the postmaster duties the same year and handled the mail until 1890, when Peter Clay took charge. C. H. Roberts was postmaster from 1891 until 1894 when Francis W. Quinn served until 1898, at which time Roberts again assumed the duties.

Roberts remained in charge until 1915, and built the first post office in 1907. This was a small building above the Bingham Merc.

C. L. Countryman became postmaster in 1915. Archie Stuart took over from 1921 to 1924 and Boyd J. Barnard served from 1924 until 1933.

W. L. James was postmaster from 1933 until 1937 when his son, Earl T. James was appointed in his place.

Amy Snow served as acting postmaster for awhile and in 1957, Ed Johnson was appointed to the post.

The post office was moved from its first location to the Society Hall down Main Street, then to the old Federal Building where it remained until the new post office was built across from the Utah Copper Hospital in 1933. It remained there until it was moved to Copperton on December 10, 1962.

The Bingham post office can claim a first and a last in U.S. postal service history.

When it was established as a rural route in 1900, it was the first such route authorized outside of a farming region. When carriers started delivering mail in the canyon, they rode over their route on horseback and Bingham was the last town in the country to deliver mail by horseback.

Thus, Irvin Stillman and Louie Kolman who still made the rounds on horseback in the late 1930's, were the last of their kind. For many years, one of the most cherished chores for boys in Bingham was the task of riding the mail horse from the livery stable on Railroad Avenue to the Federal Building in the morning so it would be available for the carrier.

Kolman was a small man with a humpback and when he loaded the mail bags around the saddle and then climbed onto the horse, it was hard to tell whether he was sitting in the saddle or in one of the bags of mail.

Other carriers who served in Bingham Canyon include Guy Baum, R. I. Farrell, Dee Johanson and Frank Shafter.

Among the long-time employees in the post office were Althea Christensen, Ivy Hull, and John Creedon.

In 1916, the rural route was discontinued and city delivery inaugurated.

The fact that Bingham Canyon's mail carrier continued to make his rounds on horseback long after other towns discouraged this means of transportation is not surprising to anyone who lived in the canyon. Bingham's mail carrier had to travel on mountain trails, go up and down gulches and in general cover one of the most exhausting routes in the service. So, the horse was the answer.

Another Binghamite who utilized the horse for his deliveries was Hugo "Nick" Newman. Nick was deaf and was given his nickname from his habit of asking for nickels when he was a young boy in the canyon. Nick rode a horse the length of the canyon to deliver the *Salt Lake Tribune* and the old *Salt Lake Telegram* to his customers.

The horse was long a part of the business life in Bingham Canyon.

A stage line once connected canyon residents with the towns in Salt Lake Valley. The horse and buggy was once the main means of transportation. Horses pulled freight, ore and delivery wagons. Thus livery stables and blacksmith shops were a necessity.

Harry Black owned a livery stable near the Rio Grande Depot. The Star livery was near the number 2 Fire Station. The Bingham Coal was in Hegland Alley. Early in the days of the mining camp there was a livery stable below Heaston Heights, across the road from where the LDS Church stood. When excavation work was taking place in the area, wagon wheels, harnesses and other evidence of a livery stable was uncovered but no one seems to know who owned it or when it was in operation.

Up in the main business district, Chandler owned the biggest livery stable in town, the Bingham Livery. It stood where the Princess Theater was built and was a huge barn housing a string of saddle horses as well as "work" animals.

The livery stables rented horse and buggies to those who couldn't afford to own or keep their own. Until train service was established, which was much cheaper and faster, the buggy rental business flourished.

A single seat buggy rented for $5 for the hour drive to Midvale. Larger ones cost $7 for the same trip and the rent for the same trip and the rent for a trip to Salt Lake City was $10. It took about three and a half hours to make the trip to Salt Lake City by horse and buggy.

One of the first Bingham-Salt Lake Stage Lines was established by Frank Leak in 1892. A round trip to Salt Lake City cost $5 and a round trip to Murray $2.50.

The railroads moved into Bingham in 1871, but it wasn't until after 1893, that they offered passenger service to towns in Salt Lake Valley. Tickets cost $2 for a trip to Salt Lake.

Even after trains took over most of the passenger service to Salt Lake, the stage business was strong in the canyon.

The train depot was on Railroad Avenue (in the beginning it was merely two box cars) and twice a day the stage would meet the train and carry the passengers from the depot up the canyon.

People would rent a saddle horse from the stables, ride to their destination, put the reins over the saddle horn, turn the horse loose and it would return to the stable on its own.

There were also ore haulage firms who contracted to haul ore from the mines to the smelter or to the railroad.

Among these were the Jimpson and Bunker Ore Haulers in the area where the Bingham Coal and Lumber Company stood. Two brothers, George and Tom Mayne, also had an ore haulage business and the Christopherson brothers were prominent in the same business.

These men owned four-horse teams that pulled the ore wagons. There was always plenty of work for them.

Among the blacksmiths in the town were Albert Marriott, Ross Marriott, Ben Cole, Ray Allan, Francis Miller, Roy Hughes, Joe Marriott and Jesse Prigmore.

As far as the young boys in the town were concerned, the most popular blacksmith was McDonald whose shop occupied the corner later taken over by the Copper King.

Ed Johnson remembers McDonald as a powerfully built man with huge biceps. "But the most fascinating feature about him was the fact he had a mouthful of gold teeth. When he hammered away at the forge, the light from the fire would make his teeth sparkle. It was a tremendous sight to watch him work while lights flashed off the gold in his mouth," Ed said.

McDonald apparently enjoyed having the town's boys watch him work. He encouraged them to hang around by taking horseshoe nails and fashioning them into rings which he gave to anyone who wanted one. He treated the boys with kindness at all times.

But the livery stable, the stage coach and the blacksmith were doomed. What the train couldn't do, the automobile did. And when the first car, believed to be owned by A. D. Heaston, made the then-arduous journey up the canyon's unpaved road before 1910, it signalled the end of one era and the beginning of another in the canyon.

In 1918, the first official notice of the change was recorded. That year the town board passed an ordinance which set the speed limit at 15 miles per hour, okayed speeding fines of from $5 to $25 and designated parking areas for cars.

The speed limit changed little over the years. Generally it was 15 miles per hour in most areas and 8 miles per hour in school zones. In the late 1930's a traffic signal system was established in the main business district with one light at the Carr Fork corner, the other down the street just above the Bingham Drug.

Because of the narrow road, driving a car in Bingham Canyon was always a test, but it was something else again in the days before 1928, when the Main Street was first paved.

In the spring and summer there were times when the road was one long mud puddle. In the winter there was no snow plow service to keep the road clear and open. The snow and ice simply piled up and the road would actually become two long ruts formed by the wheels of the cars. Drivers often had to get out a pick and shovel and dig new ruts in the ice to enable two cars to pass in opposite directions, or to get out of an extra deep hole. Even after the street was paved, chains were necessary for cars to get all the way up the canyon or to make it up one of the unpaved side roads such as Freeman Gulch or Heaston Heights.

Automobiles were expensive and owning a car in the canyon always presented extra problems such as garage space or street parking space. Yet distances were great between one section of town and another, and at least one half of the journey was always uphill, so the taxi business flourished in Bingham.

The first car appeared on the canyon road before 1910, and Parley Jones, who was at least one of the first—and also one of the last—men to operate a taxi in Bingham, remembers driving a Moline car as a taxi there in 1912.

Headquarters for the taxi drivers was the Copper King or Bingham Merc corner and competition was fierce. In addition to Jones, other men who drove taxis in the town included, Dee Adams, Roy Wilcox, Harry Goldsworthy, Joe Delaney, Mike Gavich, Pete Loverich, Spiro Vidalakis, Louis Panos, and Frank Jimenez.

Panos, Jiminez and Jones were still driving cabs in the town in the 1960's.

As the car replaced the horse and buggy on the canyon street, the garage and auto mechanic replaced the livery stable and blacksmith.

The garage owners in Bingham Canyon were all highly-respected men who contributed much to the community. Among these were C. A. (Spud) Morley who owned and operated the Canyon Motor Company at Markham and Main; Chick Adderley and Ren Nichols with their Bingham Garage and the Adderley and Nichols garage in Frogtown; Bryan Bird and the Standard Garage, and W. B. Inglesby's Bingham Gas and Oil Company.

The Bingham-Salt Lake Stage Line switched to bus service and was run by Dr. A. L. Inglesby, a prominent dentist. The stage line was operated by Lewis Brothers Stage Company.

The car and paved roads certainly changed life in the canyon, and there were probably many who were unhappy because of this.

In the first week of August, 1910, the *Salt Lake Tribune* ran a story complaining about the condition of the road leading from Salt Lake City to Bingham. The editor of the *Bingham Bulletin* reacted strongly to the story and in the issue of August 12, 1910, he editorialized:

"Last week the *Tribune* published an article denouncing the condition of the Bingham road, or rather, the road leading from the city to the camp. It is alleged that part of the road is good and part of it is bad. The bad part, so the story goes, lies between the valley and the mouth of the canyon.

"Now, according to the story, it is possible to make the entire length of the road a boulevard, and if it were made so, traffic would be increased between the two places.

"The general deductions from the article are: That if the road was put in perfect condition, the mining men would come out to camp in a hurry, more automobiles would be owned in the camp, and that the camp would become a tourist resort.

"The facts are these: Few people in the camp give a very big damn how the roads are down around the foothills. However, the roads are in such condition as will justify automobiles making the run to the city in less time than the regular train schedule. (Local auto-drivers make the boast that they beat the train going and coming from the city).

"The road is in fair enough condition for valley peddlers to come up day after day and compete with local merchants.

"More automobiles owned in the camp will mean more money spent in the city.

"Mining men come out anyway and are the last to holler.

"What Bingham needs is a high-board fence at the mouth of the canyon to keep the people home, rather than a paved road to the valley to encourage them to go elsewhere to spend their money."

There was never much reason for the people in the camp to visit the valley for goods or services. What the town didn't have was brought in by peddlers or other "routemen" so that almost everything was available.

Most of the women in town did the family clothes washing and some "took in" washing. For a while the Royal Laundry operated just below Dimas' store on lower Main, and Carl J. Meyers ran the Regal Cleaning and Dyeing Company in the upper part of town. Among the tailors was a man-about-town named Otto Kappel.

In the late 1800's, Miller's Hall, located on upper Main was a social center. Stage companies performed there and it was used for community dancing.

The first motion pictures were shown in the old Diamond Bar on upper Main Street where new movies were shown each night. The projectionist was Francis J. Quinn who remembers one woman coming to the management with a request. The lady wanted the man sitting behind her to stop chewing tobacco. "He keeps spitting on the floor and it splashes on my dress," she complained.

The Social Hall building below Fire Station Number 1 was also the Gem Theater and silent films were shown there. But it was the Princess Theater that most Binghamites will remember.

Ted Chesler and Max Brisk took over the movie business in the town in 1917. In 1920, George Chandler had his big livery stable in the upper part of town torn down and in its place he had erected a large, modern building and one of the occupants was the Princess Theater, owned and operated by Chesler and Brisk.

The first movie shown in the Princess in 1920, was "The Valley of The Giants" and starred Wallace Reid. The first talkie was shown there in 1930.

Chesler later bought out his partner and became the sole owner. After his death his son Harold took over the management until the final movie was flashed on its screen the night of September 25, 1960.

The two Royal Candy Stores were special places to the children and young people in the town. Store Number 1 was at 465 Main just below Society Hall and Store Number 2 was at 498 Main. Gus Drossos was proprietor at Number 1 and Pete Pitchos operated Number 2. There was a fountain and a popcorn machine and it was a favorite meeting place.

The Cho Cho's Chocolate Shop at 474 Main had a small dance floor and booths and was available for private parties.

There were movie houses in Highland Boy and Copperfield.

The Smith Building had a recreation room upstairs where small parties were held and some of the civic groups held their meetings.

The Society Hall was a popular place. New Year's Day dances were held upstairs there and dances and parties were regular events in the big wooden building.

Early union meetings and social events were held in the Union Hall below the Bingham Garage, but it later became an apartment house.

In Carr Fork the Swedish or Finnish Hall (it depended on who you were with) was a Temperance Hall, but was also a social center and many lively dances and parties were held there.

The Canyon Hall at the corner of Markham and Main was one of the most famous buildings in town. For years it was the social center of town with at least one dance a week held there.

It served as a schoolhouse for awhile, then was known as the Opera House where theatricals and other programs were held. The floor could be lowered or raised by jacks and could be tipped for better viewing when a show was presented. When used for dancing or roller skating the floor was level and rested on springs. The spring floor was the first of its kind in Utah.

In turn, C. L. Countryman, Mrs. Bebb and Tom Dafnis operated a small store in the lower part of the hall and the Utah Power and Light offices were on the ground floor for awhile.

For awhile the Canyon Garage was in the lower half and in 1937, C. E. (Spud) Morley bought the building and expanded the garage to use the entire building.

There was the Civic Center and Highland Boy's Community House.

But, from the time it was opened in 1924 until it was turned into office space by Kennecott Copper Corporation in the 1950's, the R. C. Gemmell Memorial Club was the recreational center for most of the town's inhabitants.

The Utah Copper Company built the Gemmell Club to supply recreational facilities for its employees but everyone in Bingham became familiar with the big building in Carr Fork where old-timers remember the Shawnut Mill once stood.

Men sat in the huge stuffed chairs and read papers or magazines while others sat at the card tables in the big reading room. On the walls were trophies of big game hunts. Brass spittoons were placed around the room. It was masculine and earthy and warm and welcome.

Adjoining the card room was a gymnasium with a balcony and a stage. In addition to sports events, Gemmell Club dances were held there and they were all community-wide affairs.

Downstairs was a locker room, a bowling center with two lanes, then a pool and billiards room. A boxing and wrestling ring was located in a small room near the billiards area.

Then there was the boarding house. Perhaps this establishment contributed more to the development of Bingham Canyon as a community than any other single institution.

The reason is simplicity, itself. Bingham existed because of the mines. The mines needed men and the men needed a place to live close to where they worked. But they needed more than just shelter. They needed warmth and food and drink and companionship and help and services.

They found all this in the boarding house.

Usually the boarding houses were built near or actually on the mining property. Many of them were company homes, that is, they were built and maintained by the mining company where they were located. But most of them were run by individuals, either to supplement the husband's income from the mine or, in many cases, by widows to whom the boarding house was the only source of income.

Either way, the boarding house became a center of activity in its area. Most of them had a large dining room that was heated by a pot-bellied stove. Here is where the dances and parties were held and here men gathered to talk and argue. Sometimes the arguments became heated and were settled outside in rough and tumble brawls.

Many of the boarders were single men, but there were also many married men who had left their wives and families elsewhere while they worked in the mines to earn enough money to bring them there and establish a home in the canyon.

The boarding house proprietor not only did the cooking, washing, and ironing, she had to serve as doctor, nurse, banker and minister to the men in her care.

In the early days Bingham had no hospital and at times only one doctor. The boarding house served as a hospital and many emergency operations were performed in the kitchen or dining room with a flickering lamp the only light. Many landladies, using practical knowledge in place of technical skill, nursed an injured or sick miner back to health.

Many miners found a wife in the boarding houses when a romance developed between boarder and waitress or even boarder and landlady.

Men working in the Utah Copper Mill and on the railroad, lived in a boarding house at Dry Fork. In lower Bingham boarding houses were operated by Mrs. West, Mrs. Edwin Davis, Mrs. Tom Mayne and Mrs. Sally Bracken. The Bracken boarding house was located at the mouth of Freeman Gulch.

One of the best known of the boarding houses was the Elmerton Hotel in Markham Gulch. It was close to the Canyon Hall where many musicals and plays were staged so the Elmerton became a popular stopping place for actors. It was also in the center of town so many salesmen used it as a headquarters.

Farther up town was the Bingham Hotel operated by Mrs. Oddie. Near the Bingham Meat Market was a two story boarding house which had several owners over the years including Mary Bianco and Carlotta Moretti.

The Roberts Hotel was in the center of the main business district. On upper main were Jim Rolando's California Rooms.

Copperfield had the Utah Copper Club House and the Rex Hotel. The Rex was a big building right at the entrance to the town and was called "The Big Ship." Theo Schweitzer was an early manager and the last manager before it was razed was Earl Nepple.

Other boarding houses in Copperfield were run by the Byrnes, Wilson, Fox and McDonald families. There was a large boarding house at Telegraph and the U.S. Mines had one in the South Galena area. Later it was moved to Copperfield and among its managers were Ollinger, Wetzel, Bill McIvor and Bud Starley. There was the B&G boarding house operated by Mrs. Michael Creedon. There was a boarding house in the center of Jap Camp and one in Greek Camp.

Carr Fork had several boarding houses, probably more to the square foot than any other area in the town.

There was the Grand Hotel run by Mrs. Annie Dahlstrom, Mrs. Fannie Johnson, Mrs. Charles Johnson, Mrs. Joe Geisler and Mrs. O. D. Baker.

There was The Garadice, built by Barney Quinn and named after his birthplace in Ireland. There was Mrs. Roper and her Do-Drop Inn, Mary Sams and the Cyprus Hall. Mrs. Beth Murphy operated one of the last boarding houses in the area, at the foot of the B & G tram. A Japanese family ran a boarding house where the Gemmell Club was built. The Eagle Hotel was across the street from the tram.

There was a boarding house at Cottonwood Gulch above Carr Fork when there were several small mines in operation there. There was the Apex boarding house and Mrs. Joe Melich (mother of Mitch Melich, the uranium millionaire who ran for governor in Utah on the Republican ticket in 1964) ran a boarding house in Phoenix. Mary Sam also had a boarding house there after the fire of 1932, but later moved to Bingham.

One of the first boarding houses was run by Grandma Schoville well before 1900.

There were many others in the Highland Boy region. They were run by Hervilla, Johnson, Harry Garvin, Andy Kreasen, Mrs. Beck, Mrs. Alma Jones. There was the St.

Bernard Hotel. Manuel Suseata and Joe Useabego had boarding houses on the Minnie Road. In Doty Gulch were McKenzies, Doty's Knowly and Van Newland. There was the Clipper Club and Boston Con Number 2.

Mrs. Stephan operated a boarding house at the New England mine and the Boston Con area had the Boston Con Number 1, Alta Club, Jap Camp and Korean Camp. The McDonald place was in Doty Gulch and was hit by the snowslide of 1926.

There were also boarding houses at the Brooklyn, Yosemite, and Fortuna mines on the east slope of Bingham Canyon which were served by pack mule from Lark.

The price was always right at the boarding houses. At most places room and board cost the men $20 a month which entitled them to all the food they could eat. The plates were always piled high with food. There were no good means of storing food so it all went onto the table.

If the boarding house supplied Bingham Canyon with much of its stability in the early going, it was the saloon which supplied it with much of its reputation.

There was never any of the speakeasy atmosphere in Bingham. Not even during prohibition was it necessary to knock on a door and say, "Joe sent me."

Bingham Canyon had everything and did everything in the open. In the early days there was a bar in practically every store, even the ones that catered almost exclusively to women. And it is reported that at one time there were 29 saloons operating in the canyon.

Gambling operated openly in many of the saloons. Card games, roulette and craps were played and money constantly changed hands at the tables in the saloons.

Among the saloons were the Copper King, The Pastime, The Diamond, The Mascot, The U.S., The Butte, The Senate,

The 16-1, The Tivo 1, The Farmans, The Liberty, The Europe, The Moonlight Gardens, The Starlight Gardens, The Copper Gate, The Italian French Bar, The Combination Bar, The International Club, The Rendevu, The Monarch.

Three of the better known saloons were The Diamond, The Pastime, and The Copper King.

Dr. Flynn bought the Pastime for his brother and the Copper King was built by the Fisher Brewery with Bill Jones as the owner. The Methodist Church was originally behind the Copper King so Jones bought it and had a new church building erected in the area below the Bingham Central School where there were no saloons in the immediate vicinity.

Along with the saloons there were several pool halls. There was a pool hall in the building where Tom Praggastis had his store in Frogtown. There were pool tables in the Diamond Bar. Foote had a pool hall in the Freeman area and there was Berger's Nest in the main district.

Built by Joe Berger, the Berger's Nest was one of the most popular places in town.

Another open secret in Bingham Canyon was the Red Light district. Prostitution existed in the town and was licensed and regulated after the town was incorporated in 1904.

After ore was discovered in the canyon and the digging began, there were few women in the canyon. In this world of mostly men—and many of them hard-working and hard-drinking men—it follows that prostitution would become one of the first trades plied there.

The first brothel, called "The Chicken Ranch," was located in upper Main near the Starless mine on the road to the Copperfield region. A second house opened across the street and was called "The Mountain Home."

With this start, upper Main became the Red Light district although there was a district in Frogtown.

The district was referred to as "The Line" and usually the inhabitants of "The Line" stayed there and had little contact with the rest of the town.

An exception to this were the days when the girls were "paraded" down to the doctor's office for their medical examination. Mostly, the other women would stay indoors during the procession, but a few would come out and heckle the business girls. One old-timer remembers that usually the prostitutes were silent and ignored the taunts, but occasionally one would answer back. He recalls one shouting, "If it wasn't for your husband, I wouldn't be here," to one of the hecklers.

Later the district was located at 520 Main Street and everyone in town knew the address and the business that was conducted there.

The girls went by first names only and these names, too, were familiar through the grapevine that exists in all small towns.

One of the madams, Dorothy, drove a white Cord, and had outside interests such as belonging to the Bingham Gun Club where she was a respected member.

The saloons, the gambling, and the red light district gave Bingham Canyon a reputation as a wide open city and in that respect it was. Growing up in the town, most boys and girls were aware of what went on, but it all took place apart from their lives and they had tolerance without participation.

In most respects, Bingham Canyon had as ordinary a daily life as any other small community. It carried on business as usual in unusual surroundings and with a population that was extraordinarily metropolitan for any Western town. But it did carry on normally.

For example, on almost any week day after 1920, by the time the business district in Bingham Canyon was starting to unlock its doors for the morning trade, Harley (Huck) English was already making his second trip through town.

Huck had driven his pickup truck from the small dairy at the mouth of Dry Fork and turned onto the canyon road before daylight. He had gone up the canyon delivering milk to his customers and now was on his way home. As he drove down the canyon he stopped at each cafe and picked up a can of garbage. When he had completed his garbage collection, he drove back to the dairy and used the garbage to feed the pigs he raised in pens along the base of the hills.

Huck English was born in the house at the dairy. His father had run a merry-go-round where the barn now was, then had moved the ride to the Frogtown area in Bingham Canyon. In 1920, Huck started in the dairy business.

Beer and whiskey were not the only liquid refreshments available in the canyon.

There were, also, many dairies and supplying the demand for milk was always a profitable business in the town.

George and Matilda Johnson did not stay long in the cabin at South Galena after Ed was born. Like many miners of that time, George moved from mine to mine, looking for better working conditions, a dryer and safer tunnel, richer strike.

George worked in several mines in the Copperfield area, the family moving from frame house to frame house to be close to the tunnel each time he changed jobs. Eventually they moved to Bingham where George went to work in a mine in Markham Gulch.

In 1896, a fire destroyed most of their belongings and the family moved to Carr Fork eventually settling at 69 Carr Fork.

At this time they went into the dairy business. They had five cows which were kept in a big barn and George would deliver the milk to their customers in five gallon lard buckets, pouring the milk from the buckets into a container furnished by the customer.

One of Ed's customers was Francis W. Quinn who enjoyed teasing the boy. "Tell your mother she is putting too much water in the milk," Quinn said. Ed relayed this to his mother who said in a strong Swedish accent.

"All right. No more milk for the Quinns." And for her the matter was closed.

When Quinn found his milk supply shut off, he went to Matilda, apologized sincerely explaining he was joking. Only then did she relent and consent to sell milk to the Quinns again.

There were several dairies in lower Bingham including one at the border of Frogtown and Railroad Avenue. There was a dairy on Hegland Alley. There was a dairy at Lead Mine. A Turner family herded their cows to the mountains above Telegraph in Copperfield where spring water was available, kept them there every summer and delivered milk to residents of the area. In the fall the family would take the cows down Butterfield Canyon, to Bluffdale for the winter, but they continued delivering milk to their customers by horse and wagon.

There were several Greek dairies. The Condas Dairy was located on the old road below the canyon. "Jimmy the Goat Man" had a dairy that supplied customers in Bingham Canyon.

Then there was Hogan Dairy in West Jordan which had a huge business in Bingham. Glen Hogan's father started the dairy, then Glen and his sons and grandsons continued the business.

There was the Three-Bar Dairy in Lehi with a route in Bingham.

In the early days when Bingham was a mining camp, and early in the 1900's, several families kept their own cows and an area in Markham was known as "cow flats."

And the women of Bingham Canyon had more things to be concerned with than whether there was or was not a Red Light District in the town.

In 1907, the Women's Civic Club was organized and immediately tackled such projects as welfare for the poor, playgrounds for the children, and a library.

Residents of the mining town had a reputation for taking care of their own problems and when the women felt a library was needed they went after it.

The minutes of the town board's meeting on March 10, 1920, has the following entry:

"Mrs. A. C. Cole, Mrs. Ed Heather and Mrs. Thomas Nerdin of the Women's Club appeared before the board in relation to the establishment of a public library, and asked for the board's aid in establishing such a library. The town authorized the construction of necessary shelving in a room given by the Commercial Club and otherwise agreed to assist in the furnishing and equipping of said room."

That accomplished, the women launched a community-wide drive for books. People were asked to give spare books to the library and the Boy Scouts served as the collection agency.

The Women's Club also asked for money to purchase new books and a start had been made toward getting a library.

At first there were only the shelves where the books were kept. There were no reading rooms, tables or chairs. The library opened two nights a week at which time books could be checked out. Mrs. Nerdin and Mrs. Coles donated their services as librarians.

The next big push for a library resulted in a setback for the women. On January 25, 1928, a special election was held, at the request of the club, to let the voters decide: "Shall the town of Bingham establish and maintain a free public library, and levy a tax of one mill on the dollar for the purpose of maintaining the same?"

It suffered an overwhelming defeat, 98 against and 17 for.

The town board softened the blow by voting to contribute $30 a month to help maintain a library and agreeing to partition off the court room with one room to be used as the library. A salary of $5 per month was set for the librarian.

When the Depression hit, the $30 was reduced to $15 and remained at that figure for some time. By 1938, there were a thousand books in the library and the Women's Club continued to aid in its growth.

Among the women who served as president of the Women's Club through the late 1930's, were: Mrs. J. B. Myers, Mrs. A. C. Cole, Mrs. Eugene Morris, Mrs. Eugene Chandler, Mrs. Will Myers, Mrs. Bert Roberts, Mrs. James Nerdin, Mrs. Edwin Johnson, Mrs. Ted Chesler, Mrs. C. L. Countryman, Mrs. Joe Kemp, Mrs. W. H. Harris, and Mrs. S. J. Grandquist.

While the Women's Club enjoyed a long life, the first men's club was short-lived.

The first men's civic group in Bingham was the Commercial Club, also organized in 1907. It was reputed to be a private gambling club, but it did become involved in civic affairs.

The club rooms were originally located over Bourgard's Butcher Shop where the post office was built, but later moved to Miller's Hall.

The clubhouse included card rooms billiard rooms and a bar. Its membership included most of the business and professional men in the town.

In 1920, the club ran into hard times, disbanded and no attempt was ever made to form it again.

But Bingham had a list of civic organizations with long and distinguished records of service to the community. The Kiwanis Club was active from 1923 until 1936. The Junior Chamber of Commerce promoted the first Galena Days celebration in 1939. The Lions, Eagles and Elks had chapters in town. The Firemen were always active in community affairs.

There were four churches in the community and all played active, vital roles in the development of the town and its citizens.

In Highland Boy the Methodist Community House Center was open to everyone regardless of religion or ethnic background and, as its name implies, it was a center of activity for the people in the region.

The Swedish Zion Lutheran Church and the Holy Rosary Catholic Church were located in Carr Fork. The Methodist Community Church was near McGuire's Gulch in central Bingham and the Church of Jesus Christ of Latter-day Saints ward house was on the hillside just above Heaston Heights.

On October 18, 1940, the last giant smokestack of the old Yampa Smelter in Frogtown was dynamited. More than 100,000 bricks in the 125-foot chimney were donated by Utah Copper Company to be used in constructing a new LDS ward house in Copperton.

It was Brigham Young, President of the LDS Church, who first sent the Bingham brothers to the canyon in the West Mountains and the church always played an important role in the town.

In 1896, a Sunday School was held in Bingham under supervision of the South Jordan bishopric. The meetings were held in the 43rd district school house each Sunday afternoon and teachers were listed as Hanna Peck, Eliza McNeil, Rachel Mayne, Minnie Gough and Dorlesca (Phillips) Kenner. The records list some of the individuals who attended meetings then as Neva E. Lee, Morris Lee, Ray Mayne, Florence Mayne, Mamie Forbes, Thomas Priday, and W. W. Beckstead. Neva Lee was secretary.

In 1899, a small chapel was built and on October 1, 1899, the Bingham LDS Ward was organized under the direction of Angus Cameron and Charles W. Penrose. William Thompson became the first bishop, N. C. Hair was sustained as First Counselor, William B. Waters, Second Counselor and R. T. Jones, clerk.

N. C. Hair was superintendent of the Sunday School with Reese T. Jones, First Counselor, Cyril Peck, Second Counselor, William Thompson led the choir and Mamie Brink was organist.

On September 16, 1900, the first Relief Society was formed with Christine Brink, President, Harriett Jones, First Counselor and Lottie Waters, Second Counselor.

From 1902 to 1906, a Sunday School was held in Highland Boy under W. N. Hair and Thomas Hair. And for a short time in 1900, a Sunday School was held in Copperfield. This was soon discontinued but it was revived again later under David C. Lyon and services were held in the Copperfield School.

Among the men who served as bishop of the ward over the years were: William Thompson, William Waters, James A. Wright, David C. Lyon, Clinton S. Robison, Wilford H. Harris, Ira E. Moss and Edwin W. Johnson.

In June, 1961, the last meeting was held in the ward and the officers were released from their duties.

The first Methodist Church was built in Bingham Canyon in 1874. At first the Methodist Church was situated on upper Main Street, but was moved to a location just below McGuire's Gulch in central Bingham.

In March, 1899, a bell was purchased and installed in the belfry of the Methodist Church and when the church was moved to its central location the bell continued to ring every Sunday morning to call its members to worship.

Services were held there until May, 1957, when the Bingham Canyon church was combined with the Copperton Community Methodist Church and the furnishings were transferred from the Bingham church to Copperton.

Many Binghamites can remember attending services or going to school in the Bingham Canyon Methodist Church and the church bell was a familiar sound every Sunday. The Reverend Meredith Smith was among the pastors who were in charge of the Bingham Methodist Church.

The Highland Boy Community House, a project of the Utah Mission of the Woman's Society of Christian Service, served that district of the canyon for many years and was open to all people regardless of color, race or religion.

After the Bingham church transferred to Copperton, the Community House moved into the Bingham church building where it remained until later in 1957, when the Community House also combined with the Copperton church and the name was changed to the present St. Paul's Community Methodist Church.

Shortly after he took charge of the Utah mission in 1871, the Reverend Patrick Walsh visited the mining camp in Bingham Canyon and from then on the Catholic Church played an important part in the life of the town.

In 1873, Father Scanlon succeeded Father Walsh and was so impressed with Bingham Canyon that he proposed building a church there. However, it was not until May of 1890, after Father Scanlon conducted Mass in the town, that a subscription list was formed and the first step toward building a church was taken.

Barney B. Quinn donated property in Carr Fork and a frame building was erected there. Services were held there the first Sunday of each month.

By 1902, the congregation outgrew the small church and plans were made to replace it with a larger one. The new church was completed and opened in 1907.

In October, 1910, Bingham became a separate parish with the Reverend Timothy Brennan as its first resident pastor.

On Sunday, October 30, 1910, Bishop Scanlon dedicated the church in honor of the Holy Rosary.

After dedication of the church, the people of Bingham built a home for Father Brennan. The work was directed by John Palmer and was completed in January, 1911.

Father John J. Sullivan was the last pastor to serve the Holy Rosary Parish, and had the longest term of service there, 11 years, leaving in June, 1966.

The Holy Rosary Church was sold in 1958, and Father Sullivan moved the church into the BCO Hall on Main Street.

There was this thing about the doctors in Bingham Canyon—they made house calls.

In the early days they had to. Frequently there was only one doctor in town and his patients were scattered all over the canyon. He had no hospital, as such, and he made his rounds on horseback or by horse and buggy.

Dr. Wood was the first physician in town with Dr. Lamb arriving soon after. Ed Johnson remembers that when he was a young boy Dr. Lamb did not practice but spent most of his time in the saloons. Yet, when Ed came down with pneumonia, Dr. Lamb took charge and pulled him through his illness. Dr. F. J. Flynn and Dr. F. E. Straup were prominent physicians and politicians. Dr. Straup was the U.S. Mine and Highland Boy Mine physician. Dr. Flynn was the Apex Mine physician and Dr. D. H. Ray was the Utah Copper doctor.

In 1918, Dr. Russell G. Frazier arrived in town to assist Dr. Ray and later Dr. Frazier took over the Utah Copper Mine position. One of his associates and a long-time Bingham physician was Dr. Harold H. Jenkins.

In 1923, Dr. Paul S. Richards came to Bingham to take over the U.S. Mine position and he also took over the Bingham Hospital which had been started by Dr. Straup. Dr. Meyer Smernoff assisted Dr. Richards in the Bingham Hospital.

Dr. Frazier and Dr. Richards both took active roles in the community and both made important contributions to the medical profession.

Under Dr. Richards' direction, the Bingham Hospital was expanded and earned a reputation as one of the best hospitals in the region. Dr. Richards developed new techniques in back surgery and these methods were adopted around the world. Specialists from all parts of the world came to Bingham Canyon to learn Dr. Richard's technique.

One of Dr. Richards' daughters, Lenore, became the first woman surgeon in Utah and the two became partners in the Richards Clinic in Salt Lake City. Since her father's death, Dr. Lenore Richards has directed the clinic herself.

Dr. Paul Richards also served as president of the Jordan School District and was instrumental in having the high school built in Copperton.

Dr. Frazier was a civic leader and sportsman in Bingham Canyon for years, but he claimed the world's attention when he was selected as the senior medical officer with Rear Admiral Richard E. Byrd's expedition to the antarctic in 1938-'41.

While on this expedition, Dr. Frazier conducted many experiments on man's reaction to cold and made an important discovery in the treatment of diabetes. For his work there he was given a special congressional medal on September 25, 1947.

CHAPTER FIVE

THE JOURNEY BEGINS WITH 100 STEPS

THERE WERE EXACTLY 100 steps leading up the hill to the frame home behind the Belmont Hotel on Bingham Canyon's upper Main Street. Judy Arigoni had counted the steps often. She made a game of counting them as she and her half-sister, Rena Perelle, carried the wash down the steps and loaded it onto the small wagons they used to deliver the bundles of clean clothes to their mother's customers.

On the boardwalk that covered the sewer there, the girls walked past the shop operated by a Chinese businessman called, "Charley The Chink." Here the sisters played another game. They stuck their heads inside the room and shouted in shrill, young voices: "Ki yi, mucka ti."

They had no idea what the words meant, if anything. But they knew the result. As soon as the last word faded, they were running down the street, the wagons bouncing behind them, with Charley, scowling and shouting in rapid-fire Chinese, in pursuit.

The chase never lasted long and soon the girls stopped running and continued down the street without even looking back.

Judy, Rena, and their older brother, Dominick, had helped their mother for as long as they could remember. In addition to collecting and delivering the washing, they took the wagons and walked along the open levels of the mine during summer days picking up pieces of coal. Many of the children and women of Bingham performed this chore as they stored coal for the cold months. They also picked up old railroad ties and carried them home to be cut and placed in the wood pile. Old women in shawls carrying buckets of coal, or a railroad tie, were a familiar sight on the levels of the Utah Copper Company's open pit mine.

When not carrying wash or collecting fuel, Dominick, Rena and Judy helped scrub the rooms and walls in the tiny house on the hillside.

Their mother was a small, wiry woman with a tremendous inner strength that was not shown in her slight body. As Domenica Magnino, she had come from Italy to Utah in 1913, where she met an Italian miner, Dominick Perelle, married him and went with him to the mines in Panesdale, Michigan. There, Dominick Jr. was born and when he was a year old the Perelles returned to Utah going to Bingham Canyon and settling in the Highland Boy region.

In Highland Boy, Rena was born, and then the family divided. Dominick (Sr.) was what they called a "boomer miner." He wouldn't work in one mine longer than a month or two and this constantly switching of jobs tore at Domenica until she obtained a divorce.

Not long after the divorce, Domenica married another Italian miner, John Arigoni, and it was from this union that Judy was born.

When Dominick was in third grade the family moved from Highland Boy to the house behind the Belmont.

The house was small, and dark because few of the rooms had windows that looked out at the canyon. They had neighbors in houses on up the hill and sometimes tempers flared as the woman directly above tossed garbage down into Domenica's yard. But it was a big step up from what she had known in Italy and Domenica made it into a home for her three children.

The wooden floors were scrubbed constantly until Dominick complained that they should be painted black.

Every Saturday night was bath night. Domenica heated a tub of water on the coal stove in the kitchen and the children took turns bathing in the same water. So that each would have a turn at the clean water, the order of the bath was rotated each week. There was a trap door in the kitchen that led to a small underground pantry. When one of the children had a loose tooth that needed pulling, Domenica tied one end of a piece of string to the tooth and the other end to the open trap door. Then she would slam the door shut to extract the tooth.

When he was 15, Dominick wanted to do more than deliver wash to help the family financially and asked permission to quit school and take a job on the hill.

"All they teach in the school is dancing and kissing, anyway," he told his mother.

Domenica, her children and husbands, were typical of the residents of Bingham Canyon. They helped convert that rugged mining camp into a family-oriented community that was one of the most metropolitan towns in existence.

They came from everywhere. From many sections of Utah and the rest of the United States. They came from the British Isles. They came from Italy. They came from what are now the Balkan States. They came from the Scandinavian countries. They came from China and from Japan and from Korea. They came from Greece. They came from Mexico and from Spain. Later they came from Puerto Rico and during World War II many Navaho Indians came to the town to work in the mines.

At first they gathered in their own districts in the narrow confines of the canyon.

The Japanese settled in Jap Camp and the Greeks in Greek Camp in Upper Bingham. The Italians and Mexicans settled on Main Street. The English, Irish and Scotch settled in Copperfield. The men and women from the Balkans settled in Highland Boy and the Scandinavians in Carr Fork.

There they moved into the new world while keeping a tight hold onto their old world language and customs. It was never easy. At first the mining was almost exclusively in the hundreds of dark tunnels where conditions were bad and the pay was low. The miners were poor and they struggled. Inevitably, there were labor disputes and strikes. Some of the old country dislikes and distrusts continued and there was bad blood and fights.

Over the years there were many strikes, the first big one coming in 1912, but no lasting hatreds or bitterness or continued violence developed. The opening of the Yampa Smelter below the city limits in 1904 helped increase the population in Frogtown. When the smelter closed in 1912, some of these people moved farther up town.

Disasters—fire, flood and snowslide—forced many residents to relocate in other sections of the town. The centering of the mines into one huge open cut hill enabled many others to move to more desirable locations in the canyon. And, gradually, this inter-mingling did away with the suspicion and hatreds. Old wounds healed and the camp became a community.

Ned Gaythwaite, an early miner who was known for his gentlemanly manner and military bearing, came from

England to live at Number 10 Freeman Gulch, and he used to sum up the population of the town by saying, "It's a bloody League of Nations."

It was. In Bingham's League of Nation's mingled such names as: Adams and Abeyta, Allen and Ausich, Andreason and Anagnostakis; Bartell and Badovinatz, Braun and Ballamis, Bedont and Byrne, Bentley and Borich, Brown and Bernardo, Bee and Bracken; Carter and Carrigan, Cheever and Callas, Carlson and Chanak, Caulfield and Compagno, Culleton and Cunliffe; Decol and Dispenza, Densley and Durnford, Draper and Doyle; Eden and Erickson, Evans and Espinosa, Eastman and Epis; Forsberg and Fernandez, Farnsworth and Furgis, Fassio and Faddis; Garcia and Gleason, Golesh and Goff, Gerbic and Groves, Georgelas and Gavrilovich; Hatch and Horn, Harker and Herrera, Henson and Hiatt, Huebner and Hatfield; Iasella and Isbell, Ishimatsu and Ireland, Ikei and Ivie; Jensen and Jiminez, Jenkins and Jackson, Johnson and Jacques, Jones and Jimas; Krueger and Kenner, Kite and Kopesac, Koukles and Kliebenstein; Leatherwood and Lopez, Lombardi and Larick, Lipsey and Levantis; Manos and MacNeil, Marks and McCluskey, Massa and Mochizuki, Montoya and Mangrum, Markovitch and McConnell; Nelson and Neria, Nepolis and Nichols, Norton and Nielson, Nell and Nix; Osoro and Overson, Ogawa and Oliver, Ortego and Oseguera, Olson and O'Mally; Pollock and Pantalone, Poulsen and Preloran, Pett and Pino, Peterson and Pappanikolas, Petric and Pumphrey, Pagnotta and Pazell; Rice and Rubich, Rogerson and Rawlings, Ray and Rubalcava, Robison and Rasmussen; Saltas and Sullenger, Speros and Stringham, Serassio and Sorenson, Scroggin and Suzuki; Tibble and Trujillo, Tregaskis and Timothy, Toy and Tangaro, Tobiason and Thompson, Thomas and Themakes; Uzelac; Vlasic and Vranes, Valdez and Vietti, Vardakis and Vasquez; Whetzel and Wells, Watkins and Webb; Xanthos; Yengich and Zdunich, Zaccaria and Zeiser.

In the early days of the mining camp, a huge rock blocked the center of the canyon floor at about the site of the Civic Center. Wagon drivers drove around both sides of the rock and thus created the only two-way road in the canyon. But, as traffic and population increased, the rock had to be removed and Bingham's two-way wagon road disappeared.

Change was a way of life in the canyon. Old-timers remember the aerial tramway that carried buckets of ore from Highland Boy to the tram houses in Frogtown. Francis J. Quinn, Ed Johnson, George Dahlstrom and Ev Cowdell all talked about the tramway. They remembered Joe Ruttles as the boss of the tramway and said he rode the buckets twice a day. They said the low spot the tramway passed was on the B&G hill. There the boys could catch a bucket for a ride but they had to get off at the next stop or go high over Markham Gulch. Dahlstrom recalled the day when one of the boys rode a bucket over Markham. "When the bucket he was in was half-way across the gulch the tramway stopped as repairs were made higher up. We thought he would drop out and be killed but the repairs were made and he got across safely," Dahlstrom said.

A safety net was strung over the Canyon Hall School to catch any spillage from the buckets.

Over the years, mines, mills and smelters came and went and the men who worked them came and went.

In Carr Fork there was an old Swedish miner named Gust Loma who stayed in his tiny shack in the upper part of the fork. Loma would set a tin pail in front of his shack each morning and the miners who passed there on the way to work, each put part of their own lunch into the pail and this provided the old man with food.

There was a miner called, "Gus Broken Nose" whose face had been deformed as the result of an accident in a mine.

Another old miner had dug a series of holes on the Carr Fork hills and he would move his living quarters from hole to hole. The boys in the area were afraid of him and the old man lived the life of a hermit in his diggings.

A man known as "Paddy The Priest" worked as a swamper in boarding houses, hotels and saloons in the Highland Boy region. He claimed to be of royal birth and said he had once been a priest.

A character known only as "Killum-Cow Charley" worked in Bourgard's slaughterhouse in Frogtown. Killum-Cow never took a bath on purpose and his body, hair and clothes were matted with dried blood. Some of the young boys—many of whom worked in the slaughterhouse in return for a heart, kidney or piece of liver—believed that he was of royal heritage and that he came from Europe before settling at Bourgard's, but Ed Johnson, who knew him well, says that Charley never made such a claim.

Old-timers remember Dave Wheret as the strongest man in town. Dave was a huge, gentle man with tremendous strength and pride. When the Women's Whist Club held its weekly meetings, the members refused to go through the town unless Dave served as their driver. He was never defeated in a fight and his services were in demand in the rugged mining community. But the day finally came when he could no longer work and he had to go on relief. He couldn't read or write and when he was approached to fill out the necessary forms to put him on welfare, he balked.

"Does this mean I can't work anymore?" he asked.

Finally, he put down his X and went on relief. He died after slipping on a stretch of ice on upper Main and hitting his ribs on the curb when he fell.

In the early years of the town, a miner named McGee was injured in an accident and Dr. Straup performed his first amputation, taking off McGee's right leg just below the knee.

McGee was fitted with a wooden peg leg and was always known from then on as "Peggie" McGee. He had to quit mining and for awhile he drove the team and wagon that carried children from Highland Boy to school in Bingham. Then he worked around the livery stables. In the early 1920's, he slept in a hay loft across from the Bingham Garage. He would rise at the same time every morning and walk up town to get breakfast, his peg leg tapping on the wooden sidewalk. Men who slept in rooms beside the street, would use this tapping as an alarm clock, because the old miner never varied the time of this walk by more than a few seconds.

"Pinky" Lee was another familiar figure in the town. Pinky had an extremely light complexion, sandy hair and eyebrows, and "pink eyes." He was a handyman and made a living going around house to house fixing anything that needed repair. He would carry his soldering iron and other tools in a satchel and make his rounds. He was also an expert safe opener and whenever a bank vault or the safe in a store needed opening, Pinky would be summoned and sometimes he would work patiently for hours at a time, turning the knobs, his ears listening to the tumblers until the door opened.

Two other men with unusual occupations in the early days were known only by the names of Jim and Booth. These men had a water route. Each morning they went to the Bourgard Springs (where the apartments were later), filled five gallon cans of water, attached them to poles which they slung over their shoulders and then delivered the water to their regular customers in the town. The two men went out of business in about 1905, and no one seems to know what happened to them.

Life in the town was always informal and for many years this informality extended to the Utah Copper Mine, the town's largest employer.

Louis Buchman was the general manager of the mine for many years and he knew most of the miners under him by their first names. One day Buchman was walking down the center of a railroad track on one of the mine's open levels when an electric train approached rapidly.

The engineer blew his whistle, but Buchman continued to walk in the center of the track. The engineer blew his whistle again, and this time the train was almost on top of Buchman. The little general manager jumped out of the way, caught hold of the steps and swung up to the train's cab.

"You would have run over me, wouldn't you," he yelled at the engineer.

"The rules say that you have to get out of the way when I blow my whistle. The rules apply to you just like they do everyone else," the hogger replied just as hotly.

Buchman laughed. "You're right. They sure do," he said, and that was where the affair ended.

On another occasion, Buchman was making his rounds of the mine when he came across one of his employees sleeping in a water shed. Buchman didn't disturb the sleeping man. Instead he took his notepad, scribbled some words on a page and placed it on the worker's chest. The note said: "Dear Don, as long as you are asleep you are still working, but the second you wake up you're fired. Go to the time clerk and get your pay."

Bingham Canyon was never a boom town where men made fabulous fortunes overnight. It was a town where there was opportunity, but it was the opportunity to earn a living and that was all its residents asked.

When the Utah Copper Mine was getting started with its novel idea of open pit mining, the individual miners were offered stock in the company as part of their wages. Not many took advantage of the offer. Most of the miners were underground men and the open pit method of mining was not acceptable.

Ed Johnson recalls his father talking about the offer and refusing to accept stock in place of cash. "My father talked it over with my mother and I can remember him telling her, 'It will never work. The problem of transporting the ore will ruin them. I don't want any stock in such a foolish idea. I'll take my pay and do my work and I just hope they don't go broke.' "

The miners weren't the only ones who refused stock in the mine. Daniel W. Heaston, one of the first babies born in Bingham Canyon, and a successful businessman, made the same mistake.

In 1900, Heaston, along with his partners, Al Killbren and Francis W. Quinn, sold Colonel E. A. Wall a 20-acre claim in the canyon. "We sold it for $2,500 cash and a $2,500 note," Heaston later told a *Salt Lake Tribune* reporter. "Col. Wall advised me to take 5,000 shares of stock in the company. I thought he was talking through his hat and I told him his note was good enough for me. When the mine began to develop, boy did we see our mistake," Heaston said.

In spite of the skeptics, the open pit mine was a huge success, of course, and as it flourished the town stabilized.

Nowhere was this stability better reflected than on Monday.

Monday was wash day in Bingham Canyon.

Bingham was a small town and was built in a canyon which meant building space was at a premium. Any place on the canyon wall that would take a house—and some places that wouldn't—had one. This meant the people were crowded together, many times literally one house on top of another. And from every house there ran one or two clotheslines.

On Monday, drying wash flew from every house and in every direction. It hung on lines running from houses to nearby telephone poles; it ran from upstairs windows up the side of the hill to trees or cribbings. It ran from porch to porch. It went uphill and downhill and it was on exhibit to everyone who came by. There were no wardrobe secrets in Bingham.

The numerous clotheslines started another tradition in the town. The Monday night before Halloween became known as clothesline night." On this night the boys of the town went around the canyon cutting clotheslines. The men and women maintained a strict watch to prevent having their clotheslines cut, but the vigilance seldom paid off. In the darkness and in the shelter of nearby houses, garages, or the canyon walls, the boys usually managed to sneak through and snip the lines. As a result most of the wire lines in the town were a series of splices and knots where repairs were made after an attack on clothesline night.

In Bingham, Halloween, itself, was a night of mischief, but it was condoned, just like clothesline night.

For many years, the outdoor toilets were the primary target, and Carr Fork residents like to recall one particular incident involving a family and its outdoor bathroom.

This privy was the property of Orange Baker and his family. A daughter, Ivy, would grow up to become Ivy Baker Priest, Treasurer of the United States under President Dwight D. Eisenhower.

Orange Baker was determined on this particular Halloween, that his outhouse would not be tipped over. To prevent it, he took a shotgun and stationed himself inside waiting for someone to try to tip it over.

But there was a traitor in the household. His son, Fernley, tipped off the raiders, who, forewarned, sneaked up, looped a rope around the building and from a safe distance pulled it over trapping Orange inside.

The Bakers were popular members of the Carr Fork community. Orange, though, was accident prone and spent a great deal of time in the hospital. During one such period, the neighbors took up a collection and gave it to Mrs. Baker who promptly took the money and tossed a party for the entire neighborhood.

Holidays always had a flavor of their own in Bingham Canyon.

Because it was located high in the mountains, Bingham usually enjoyed a white Christmas. Families with old-country ties combined old customs with new. In Highland Boy whole pigs would be roasted over open pits and children would dip bread into the juices and eat home-made roast pig dip sandwiches.

Bert Hocking and Herb Gust would usually dress as Santa Claus and officiate at various parties for the children. On Christmas Day, the people visited from house to house, sharing in drink and food and exchanging gifts.

All in all it was a good place to grow up. The children were allowed a great deal of freedom and much of the community life centered around their activities.

Baseball games were played wherever there was space. In Carr Fork this was in the street and when the ball went into the sewer, someone would race ahead to where there was an opening and retrieve it and play would resume. In Highland Boy, baseball was played at Frisco Flats underneath the "L" Bridge. There were better places for baseball at Bingham Central, Freeman Gulch, Railroad Avenue and Frogtown. But the creek was always a threat. In Frogtown, Elmer "Lefty" Andreason kept a flashlight and hip boots behind the bulk plant and when the ball was hit into the sewer under the railroad tracks, he would don the boots, take the flashlight and wade up the creek until he found the ball.

In the 1930's, there were street lights in most parts of the canyon, but at night most of the town was in the darkness that can be found only in the mountains. So such games as Run My Sheepie Run, Hide and Seek and Steal The Flag were big with boys and girls.

In the winter, sleighriding and skiing were popular. Bingham's sons and daughters needed only to step out of their door and they were on a sleighriding hill. In the winter they rode their sleighs down the streets of Main Street, down Markham and Freeman gulches, down Dixon and Heaston Heights. Older youths would ride bobsleds from Highland Boy down through the canyon.

Skiers, too, had their "slopes" right in their front yard, but jumping was the most popular sport with the young skiers.

In most of the houses, music played an important part. Families and friends would meet at night and sing around the piano or to the victrola. James Haun, who is known to the entertainment world as Rouvaun, spent part of his boyhood in the town. And, at Lead Mine, a tailor named Otto Kappel had two daughters, Bertha and Bessie, who were talented singers and dancers and became featured performers with the Olsen and Johnson Helzapoppin' show.

Community singing and band concerts were popular and the town had many accomplished entertainers.

A few of the town's better known singers were Annie and Phoebe (Siddoway) Masters; Beverly Clays, Blaine Wells, Joel Jensen, Deno Kannes, Betty Barnett, Gene Fifield and Eldon Tuft.

Bingham Canyon's young people responded to every call to arms during its brief history. At the start of World War I in 1918, many Binghamites enlisted and others were drafted and many served with distinction in France. The Armistice on November 11, 1918, brought about a tremendous celebration.

According to the *Press Bulletin* issue of November 15, 1918, the town was thrown wide open and "Chief of Police A. E. Paitsch, who has a son on the battle front in France asked all to enjoy themselves in the full spirit of the occasion."

The mines gave their men half a day off and the town filled with men and women celebrating the end of the war. A dance was held in the street that night, and the festivities went on for nearly a week. On November 14, the *Press Bulletin* reported a tremendous barbecue in Highland Boy saying the "patriotic Servians" put on a "genuine, old-fashioned barbecue."

But, like the rest of the nation, Bingham's joy at the ending of the great war, was offset by the flu epidemic that followed and took many lives.

In World War II practically every family in town had a son or daughter in the service and most of them became well acquainted with the efforts of Carl Zahos (Chicago Charlie) and his Victory Flag Society.

The Victory Flag Society printed several publications honoring the town's servicemen and women and kept the scattered Binghamites up to date on the home town. Officers of the society, in addition to Zahos, were: R. J. Contratto, commander; Sadie Chesler, assistant commander; Ruby Knudsen, secretary; Joseph P. Scussel, treasurer; Dale Johnston, director; Earl T. James, chairman book committee, and Shirley Jensen, typist.

Also on the home front, the workers in the copper mine were presented the Army and Navy E for Excellence award.

On the fighting front, 15 Bingham boys died. They were: Rodney Charles Davidson, Frank Hunter, William Fennemore, Rex Johnson, George Golesh, Bob Burke, Lawrence West, J. D. Smith, Delbert Dexter, Jack Whitten, Joe William Evans, Sam Tenorio, Ernest Sheen, Malcolm Rose and Theodore Dimas.

And those who returned came back to a Bingham Canyon that had already started to look at its past.

In 1939 the Junior Chamber of Commerce sponsored the first Galena Days celebration. The purpose was to honor the old-timers who had started the town and to give residents an idea of their past.

Ironically, the first child born in Bingham Canyon, Jake Hoster, died the year before. Hoster was born in a log cabin near 162 Main Street in 1869. His parents were Mr. and Mrs. Jacob Hoster and his father was one of the early prospectors and a retired soldier.

The residents celebrated Galena Days by dressing in old-time costumes, holding mucking and other mining-oriented contests, watching or taking part in a parade, a beard-growing contest (no adult male was allowed to go beardless without paying a fine for some time prior to the celebration) and dancing.

The first Galena Days proved the old-time spirit of adventure was still alive. On the morning after, Francis J. Quinn and some of the other celebrants, found the town's cafes and restaurants were too crowded to get breakfast. They got to talking and someone mentioned a place in San Francisco that served great breakfasts. So, the party drove to Salt Lake, bought plane tickets and flew to California for breakfast.

On the flight to the coast a stewardess told Quinn, "You must have the most understanding wife in the world."

Quinn asked the girl for her name and address. "I'll write and tell you if I have or not after I get home. I'll find out in a hurry."

CHAPTER SIX

TRIAL BY FIRE, FLOOD AND AVALANCHE

IT STARTED SNOWING on the weekend and continued until Tuesday. When early-risers went outside their homes in Highland Boy on Wednesday morning, February 17, 1926, the snow was up to their waists. It was particularly deep on the steep slopes of Doty Gulch where houses lined each side of the hill.

In the McDonald boarding house at the head of Doty Gulch, Nick Vlasic, a solicitor for the Slavonian Merc, was taking an order from the cook, Jose Alencia. At about 8 A.M. the two men walked from the kitchen to the meat house which was against the side of the hill. Alencia was wearing only lightweight clothing but Vlasic was dressed warmly. He had on a sheepskin coat, high boots and a cap. That fact probably saved his life.

"We had just closed the door. The lights were burning and I could see the floor coming down. We had already had several small snowslides in the area and I knew what had happened, but I didn't have time to react.

"I was pinned under the snow and the boards in an upright position, but the cook was knocked to the floor and buried. During the day I could hear him groan and I would talk to him to encourage him, but after a long time he stopped groaning and I knew he was dead.

"I was never knocked unconscious, but late in the day I went to sleep. I guess it was about 4:30 or 5 P.M. I woke up and could see light through the snow. I worked an arm loose and pushed my hand up through the snow. Someone grabbed my arm and shouted, 'Here's one and he's alive.' It was Dr. Paul Richards and there was a nightwatchman named John Danoscovich and some other men with him. My father was there. He knew I had gone soliciting door to door in the area and he had searched for me all day," Vlasic recalled from his Salt Lake City home recently.

The avalanche that roared down the gulch that day was the worst disaster in the town's history. A total of 39 persons were killed in the slide and at least 17 homes and the big boarding house were demolished.

The cook, Alencia, and his wife who was in the kitchen when the slide struck, were among those killed.

Walter Rimby was not in the house he shared with his widowed mother when the slide struck it. He hurried to the site as soon as he heard of the disaster and heard his mother scream for help. Despite the desperate efforts of Walter and the rescue party, they reached Mrs. Rimby too late. She had been trapped behind the kitchen stove and was badly burned and she died before they could free her.

Two small children were saved.

Nick Vlasic remembers two small children whose first names were Johnny and Conceta, were saved when they were buried under an overturned bathtub which left them air space and they were in good shape when they were taken from under the tub.

Ed Johnson said that shortly after the avalanche struck there was a man running down the street dressed only in his long underwear. There were stories of another man riding out the slide in a bathtub.

Jim McDonald and his wife, the son and daughter-in-law of the owner of the boarding house, were buried and injured but were rescued and survived.

The entire community joined in the rescue work and relief projects were undertaken for the survivors.

The avalanche that struck Highland Boy on that winter day was not the first nor the last disaster to hit Bingham Canyon, but it was the worst and it marked the end of Doty Gulch as a residential area.

The big fears that haunted Bingham residents were fear of fire, fear of snowslide, fear of floods and fear of disaster in the mines.

In 1885, a fire wiped out the mining camp, but the number of buildings involved was so small that the total loss was only $35,000. Another fire in 1919, destroyed 20 buildings on upper Main Street and damage was listed at $50,000.

Fire destroyed the Bourgard Butcher Shop and 11 other buildings in the area where the post office was later built, and killed two volunteer firemen on August 17, 1924.

A mud flood rolled down Markham Gulch in 1930 damaging many homes in the area.

But it was Highland Boy that bore the brunt of the major disasters. First and worst was the avalanche of 1926. Then came a fire in 1932, and another snowslide in 1939.

On the afternoon of September 8, 1932, Ann Predovich was in the kitchen of her home in Highland Boy when she heard the fire siren blow. She looked out the window, saw smoke and flames. A little later she went outside and there found "that all hell had broken loose."

"There was smoke and fire everyplace and people were hurrying from their homes carrying odd bits of personal belongings. There was a lot of crying and shouting and confusion and everyone was worried about someone who couldn't be accounted for," Ann recalls in talking about the day that everyone from Bingham refers to as "The Highland Boy Fire."

Of all the disasters, fire was the most feared. The reason was simple enough. Most of the buildings were frame and the wood was tinder-dry and unpainted. The buildings were so close together that a spark from one spread the fire to another and then another in rapid succession. Water to fight the fire could be a problem and there was the very real danger that what started as a small fire could easily become a holocaust involving the entire town.

The Highland Boy fire came close to doing just that.

The fire apparently started in the abandoned Princess Theater and the first warning was sounded at 3:20 P.M. The old theater was destroyed quickly as volunteer firemen found they did not have enough water pressure.

There was little wind blowing and no panic. Residents carried bedding and furniture and other personal belongings to cleared places and everyone thought the fire would be checked before it could spread.

But then the Jones boarding house on one side of the theater ignited and almost at the same instant the Highland Boy Merc on the up-canyon side of the theater burst into flames.

The Johnson Market on the left side started to burn and now, as Miss Predovich recalled, all hell had broken loose.

Refugees crowded the narrow street carrying their personal belongings. One woman had a pig sty. Another, Sophia

Loverich, clutched a pillow that had come from the old country.

Now a curious thing happened. The fire created its own wind and quickly spread the flames to other buildings on the street. The flight of people from the fire's path became a panic.

A total of 35 persons were burned and 300 were left homeless. Of those burned, Bincente Falzer, Tony Strelich and Mike Strelich were burned badly enough to require hospital treatment.

The Highland Boy school was destroyed. The property belonging to Mrs. Alma Jones included a 53-room house, a 38-room house and a combination dining-room and recreation-dance hall with furniture and was valued at $80,000 and was not insured.

The loss at the Highland Boy Merc was $25,000, and the Johnson Market about the same. The Bolic store and the St. Bernard Hotel, almost at the limits of Highland Boy, were burned.

The exterior property of the Utah-Delaware Mining Company, partly covered by insurance, was destroyed. This included the ore bin, spilling 400 tons of ore, the tramway and cable, snowsheds and lumber.

The other mining companies suffered loss of company-owned boarding houses and exterior equipment.

The two fire departments attempted to get through to help the Highland Boy volunteers and the mining companies. They failed to establish a line of defense, but did make a cleared and protected line of retreat which saved the people and probably the town of Bingham.

Principal F. C. Smith of the Highland Boy school, said he was glad the fire did not start sooner.

It was the first day of school and classes had just been dismissed when the Utah-Delaware fire siren gave the warning. Children from school were able to reach their homes and join their parents before they had to flee the area.

The fire line was held successfully at the Nick Bolic store down the canyon. Up the canyon the line was held at the J-Level of the Utah Copper Mine. The area in between, about one-third of a mile, comprised the business and residential section of Highland Boy.

At least a partial list of the homes and businesses destroyed in the fire includes:

Highland Boy Barber Shop, St. Bernard Hotel, Miner's Pool Hall, Strilich Mercantile Co. with an estimated loss of $20,000 and $1,000 insurance; the Sidney Tregaskis home, the Jones boarding house, the Princess Theater, the Highland Boy Merc, the Mike Yengich home, the Pete Tsouras home, the Clipper Club boarding house, the Martin Pechina home, the Jim Bianchi home, and A. J. Kresen home, the Pete Uzelac home, the Matt Blockovich home, the Pete Niksich home, the Mike Bullett home, Barney's Confectionery and Barber Shop, the Johnson Market, the Steve Kosovich home, the Mrs. George Zdunich home, the Mrs. Louise Kallen home, the Jose Salazar home, the Highland Boy School, the Mrs. Joe Vejnovich home, the Don Skala home, the Mrs. John Sarich home, the Union Pool Hall, the Mrs. Tony Azzelio home, the H.B.Z. Meeting House, the Serbian Lodge House, the Mike Zurkovich home, the Joe Birkland home, the John Pazell home, the Mike Martinez home, the Nick Bogden home, the Durant Apartments, the Berto Moretti home, the George Smiljanich home, the Pete Loverich home, the Mrs. Johanna Kascek home, and the John Stilinovich home.

Most of the homes were not replaced. The residents moved to other parts of the town where there were available houses and physical wounds of the fire healed.

Miss Predovitch recalls seeing Miss Ada Duhigg of the Community Center soon after the fire started and of seeing her frequently in the time that followed. "She was always the first on the scene in time of trouble and we regarded her as "The Angel of Highland Boy," Ann said.

Relief workers went into action quickly after the fire and were headquartered in the Community Center.

Fire was always a danger in the canyon and periodically destroyed homes and took some lives in the town. But the next big natural disaster was another avalanche.

At just about 10:25 P.M. on February 8, 1939, Mike Garcia of Highland Boy walked past the Mrs. Stana Tomas home in Central Highland Boy. The Tomas home stood in the part of town that had been the center of the 1932 fire. The house had been constructed after the fire.

A blizzard that residents later called the worst in 15 years was raging through the canyon and Garcia walked rapidly. The fact he was in a hurry might have saved his life.

Inside the Tomas home, Mrs. Tomas was in the kitchen, Duchin, 19, was asleep in a back room of the five room house. The other members of the family, Eli, 16, Nick, 22, Helen, 11, Milka, 12, and a friend, Sam Narich, 42, were in the living room playing Chinese checkers or listening to the radio.

At exactly 10:25 P.M. a neighbor, Walt Bolic, saw a flash like lightning, heard a peal like thunder and looked out the window just after the avalanche took off the top of the Tomas house. The slide wiped out the telephone service in every home in Highland Boy except the one in the Bolic residence and he quickly summoned help.

The Tomas family did not have time to know what smashed into them. Nick said afterwards, "that all of a sudden there was a big smash and snow and bricks were falling around everywhere. The lights went out and I was sailing through the air just like riding on a toboggan. I couldn't think of anything to do except I remembered that someone had told me to relax if I were ever in an accident. I tried to relax.

"It all happened so quickly, in no time at all I was thrown about 50 feet from the house. Snow was all over me. I started to dig my way out and by the time I got my head out, I saw somebody else digging out. I ran to him and it was my brother Mike. We started to look around and we dug frantically in the snow. We found George (Gerner) and he had a bad cut on his head. (Gerner was in front of the house and was caught by the slide.) We took him into the house and by that time other people were helping us and we soon found mother's body. It's all so horrible, I can't even think."

Mrs. Tomas, her daughter, Helen, and Narich were killed, but Duchin was found alive. Another man was killed in the slide. He was John Bizjack, a blacksmith, whose cabin a half-mile above the Tomas home was wiped off the mountain by the slide.

Duchin was found under about two feet of snow, still in his bed and wrapped in blankets.

Duchin was buried for 10 hours and was given up for dead. The search was conducted in front of the house when, finally, two searchers decided to probe the area where the house had stood and started digging in that area. They found Duchin and he was taken to the Bingham Hospital where he recovered.

It had been a night of good luck and bad luck for Duchin. He had survived a 10-hour burial, but he almost missed the slide entirely. Earlier he had been in Bingham with some friends who wanted to see a movie. Duchin turned down the offer to attend the movie and went home to get some sleep.

CHAPTER SEVEN

HOW THEY PLAYED THE GAME

THE BONFIRE AND PEP RALLY was held in the space before the entrance to the tunnel which was being built and would do away with the road to Copperfield. It was snowing lightly, but the flakes were big and wet and the field would be muddy on the next day. The studentbody president was Tommy Strelich, Agnes McDonald was vice-president. Cheerleaders were Lawrence Pino and Edna Smith. The principal was Tommy McMullin and Bailey Santistevan was the football coach. It was Friday night, November 18, 1938, and everyone in the Bingham Canyon area was convinced the Miners were only a day away from winning a berth in the State Class B High School football championship game for the first time in history.

True, Delta had to be disposed of first. But that would be taken care of Saturday afternoon. Bingham High School had been building toward this moment ever since Santistevan came out of Cripple Creek, Colorado, in 1928, to coach the high school football and baseball teams.

Santistevan was a fiery coach who worshipped the late Knute Rockne, and who dreamed of building a football dynasty of his own. The year before he had cut out baseball to concentrate on spring football and get ready for this year, the year he was certain would bring the Miners their first state football championship.

In four pre-season games, the Miners won three and then they bulled and passed their way through the Jordan Division without a loss to reach the semifinals which would be played the next day in Bingham's new stadium behind the school in Copperton.

It was the perfect year to come up with a big winner for the first time. Bingham fielded its first team in 1925, and prior to that fall of 1938, the Miners had played their home games on the dirt of the Copper Ball Park across from the high school. It was not a good place for football and Santistevan always called it, "Hogan's Brick Yard."

But the stadium, in a natural setting on the foothill behind the school, had been completed and opened for use that year. In league play the Miners had beaten two Class A powers, Davis and Granite, and practically everyone in the state had the Miners favored to beat Delta and go on to win the title.

It was a powerful team. The ends were Emil (Puss) Pollick and Ken (Curly) Reynolds; tackles were Ernest Sheen and John Osoro; guards were Dave Ireland and Gene Peterson and the center was Sid Tregaskis.

Quarterback was Joe Church, a powerfully-built athlete. Tailback was Joe (Air Mail) Frisch; Frank (Horse) Callen was right halfback and Elwin Winn was the full back.

Those were the days of one-way football and substitutions were few, but the Miners had capable replacements in every position.

So, that Friday night, when the pep rally included the students snake-dancing down Main Street in the snow, there was ample reason to anticipate a win against Delta.

As expected, the field was muddy for the game and things went wrong for the Miners right from the start. Bingham took the opening kickoff and started to drive downfield, but then the Miners were assessed a 15-yard penalty and they lost their momentum.

After an exchange of punts, Delta scored. In the second period, Delta recovered a Miner fumble on the Bingham one-yard line and scored a second touchdown to lead, 12-0.

Then came the final, crushing blow. Bingham had to punt and the ball was kicked straight up into the air. While the Bingham players stood around, Delta guard Roger Walker came shooting through, caught the ball in full stride and raced toward the goal line. He was caught on the 15 where he slipped in the mud, but Delta scored from there and added the extra point to lead, 19-0.

In the second half the Rabbits stopped several Bingham threats and Osoro recovered a Delta fumble to keep the score at 19-0. But then Frisch started to click with his passing game and completed three passes for 31 yards and ran for eight to put the ball on the Delta two. Callen crashed over from there and Winn converted and the score was, 19-7, and that was the way it ended although Delta was on the Miners' one-yard line when the game ended.

The loss stunned the townspeople. It couldn't happen, but it did happen. Bingham's first serious bid for a state title had ended in a crushing upset. It just wasn't possible. There was no hot time in the old town that night.

But the setback was only temporary. Bingham had lost the battle, but she won the war. The next fall, Bingham came back to win its first state championship in football and the feat was especially sweet because the Miners beat Delta, at Delta, in a semifinal game. Then, in the finals, the Miners beat American Fork, 13-0, in the University of Utah Stadium for the championship.

It came a year later than anticipated, but it came and Bingham had become a power to be reckoned with in football.

The starters for Bingham on that championship team were: ends, Ken Reynolds and Frank Nelson; tackles, Ernest Sheen and David Ireland; guards, Gordon Porter and Stanley Long; center, Joe Tibolla; quarterback was Frank Callen, halfbacks were Gordon Jensen and Charles Hudson, and fullback was Elwin Winn.

Callen scored the first Bingham touchdown when he ran back a short punt 30 yards and he scored the second on a 16 yard run after he teamed with Hudson on a long sleeper pass to set up the score.

The complete squad on that first state championship team included the 11 starters and: John Larick, Roy Mitchell, Howard Sumnicht, Russell Gust, Ken Poulson, Albino Lopez, Max Seal, Ken Davis, Joe Badovinitz, Rojeo Neria, Nick Yengich, John Curry, Sergio Alvarez, Kimmy Goff and Harold Mattice. Dee Carpenter was athletic manager, and Warren (Sunny) Allsop was assistant coach.

Two members of the team, Frank Nelson and Frank Callen, went on to win fame in college football. Nelson became one of the University of Utah's all-time great running backs as "Flitting Frankie" and then played pro ball for the Detroit Lions. Callen played for St. Mary's of California and then became a successful high school coach. Alvarez played baseball at Utah State and is a successful coach and teacher in Las Vegas, Nevada.

Bingham gained the state semifinals for the third straight year in the fall of 1940, but couldn't win and, then, in 1941, the Miners went all the way for the second time.

The 1941 Bingham team beat Delta, 25-6, in the semifinals and then downed Park City, 13-0, for the championship.

In the title game the two teams were scoreless for three quarters before Benny Culbertson smashed over from close range for both scores. Fleet Jack (Snake) Thurmond set up the second Bingham score with a 40-yard run and was a standout performer.

Members of the team were: Kenneth Toy, Dick Jones, Roy Bartell, Gurr Mangrum, Glen Sheen, Kay Nelson, Mike Churich, Marcey Martin, Billy Sullinger, Jack Gleason, Howard Atkinson, Robert Williams, Jay Eden, Joe Cavazos, Bob Nichols, Tommy Panos, Johnny Suseata, Billy Pino, Jack Thurmond, Benny Culbertson, Vernon Mattice, Joe Campagno, Lee Cunliffe, Don Crump, Tokio Isamatsu, Howard Swain, Billy Denver, Paul Clays, Gene Thomas, Paul Richards, Rollo Bianchi, and Jimmy Eppis. Clyde Nichols and Pete Dimas were managers assisted by Jimmy Brown and Bailey Santistevan Jr. Mike Tomas, who had been one of the victims of the 1939 snowslide, was studentbody president.

Tom Panos played tackle for the University of Utah and then became an official in Warshaw's Grocery chain in Salt Lake City. Clyde Nichols played fullback for Utah and became a teacher and coach. Jimmy Brown became a partner in the Stevens and Brown Sporting Goods Company in Salt Lake City. Joe Campagno was badly wounded with the marines in World War II.

In 1945, Bingham High School won its third state football championship. The Miners beat Park City, 14-6, in Ute Stadium for the championship after a bitter struggle with Tooele in the Jordan Division.

The Miners were led on the line by two fine tackles, Chris Apostol and George Kite. Other starters on the line were: ends, Ken Hall and James Rekoutis; guards, Wayne Ray and Eddie Osoro; center, Reed Schultz; quarterback was Kent Stillman; halfbacks were Bud Jones with Billy Boren and Jack Knudsen alternating at the other spot, and fullback was Bailey Santistevan Jr.

Team members included: Bill Thomas, Kenny Mattson, George Dimas, Pete Markis, Carl Hoffman, Blaine Peterson, Marvin Pullman, Raymond Draper, Nick Vidalakis, and Victor Roblez.

The next year, Bingham had Boren and Knudsen back, but they were the only regulars to return from the championship team and they weren't expected to repeat. But they did. Santistevan put back-to-back title teams together to everyone's surprise.

In their senior year, Boren was called "Mr. Outside" and Knudsen was called "Mr. Inside" after Army's great wartime running backs of Glenn Davis and Doc Blanchard.

George Dimas took over at quarterback and Karl Hoffman at halfback with Boren and Knudsen in the starting backfield. On the line the Miners had, Sam Mochizuki and Steve Hausknecht at ends; Kenny Mattson and Blaine Peterson as tackles; Gray Kenner and Amadeo Pino as guards; with Marvin Pullan at center.

The rest of the team included, Cal Nelson, Rex Leatherwood, Harry Manos, Cal Crump, Norman Steele, Gene Olsen, Bill Taylor, Jim Markis, Chris Goris, Zane Dumont, Chick Adderley, Bill Densley, Boyd Stoddard, Mickey Culleton, Dino Morreti, Vince Miola, David Gonzales, Milan Smilanich, Ren Adderley, Garland Bray and Bill Nevers.

In the championship game that year Bingham played a great Lincoln team and won the game, 13-12. Lincoln was led by its center, LaVell Edwards who now is the head coach at Brigham Young University.

From those two championship teams, Bingham's Chris Apostol went on to play at Utah State University, coach

Ogden High School to a state championship in football and then join the coaching staff at BYU. He is the owner of Patio Springs Country Club in Eden, Utah, and he left coaching to devote full time to that enterprise.

Boren became one of the University of Utah's great running backs despite his small size. He received his Ph.D. and is now superintendent of schools in Weber County. Knudsen went to SMU and is now a dentist in El Paso, Texas. Dimas graduated from the University of Utah and coached in the Salt Lake area for awhile then left to become head of the Alcoholism Foundation for the State of Oregon. Cal Crump became a coach and is now a counselor at Bingham High School. Mickey Culleton coached high school before his untimely death.

Writing about these last two championship teams for the old *Salt Lake Telegram* was a young sports writer named Steve Smilanich.

As a young boy Steve had been in the bottom apartments when the snowslide took off the Tomas residence in 1939. He wrote sports in Salt Lake, then went to New York where he was college sports editor for United Press International. He was killed in an automobile accident back there in 1971.

That 1946 title was the last in football for the Miners. Santistevan had realized his dream of building a dynasty and had won four championships, two in succession.

After Santistevan retired from coaching, the Bingham reins were taken up by a former Miner athlete, Del Schick. Schick moved to Hillcrest and is now principal of that high school.

Santistevan also coached Bingham to nine state high school and five American Legion baseball championships. Among the Bingham players who moved into professional baseball were: Gene Fish, Louis Valdez, Stanley Long and Marion Cowdell, all pitchers; Russell Gust, Don Gust, Kay Nelson and Sonny Robertson, infielders and Tommy Pazell, outfield.

Robertson played in the major leagues with the Chicago Cubs for awhile and the Gust brothers played for the old Salt Lake Bees in the Pioneer League. Pazell, a lefthander with great fielding and batting skills, was with the Boston Red Sox when he was drafted into the army in World War II. In action in Europe he was badly wounded by machine gun fire and this ended his baseball career. He is now a teacher at Bingham High School.

Another with great promise, was Ernest Sheen. Ernie was built along the lines of Babe Ruth and was a strong hitter. He was considering a professional baseball career when he went into the Army Air Corps in World War II. The plane on which he served as a gunner, never came back from a mission over New Guinea.

It was ironic that Bingham High School won many state titles in football and baseball but only one in basketball—and that one after the town was almost disbanded—because the town's first love was basketball.

Life in Bingham Canyon was always competitive, so it was natural the inhabitants would adopt athletics. The *Bingham Bulletin's* first issue in 1891, had an item that said: "Kicking the football is the chief amusement in Bingham every day between the hours of six and seven p.m. Big, little, old and young do the kicking act to perfection and seem to enjoy it."

Over the years, Bingham's big and little, old and young, played many games to perfection and always enjoyed it.

But it was in 1917, when the high school gymnasium was built, that the town fell in love with basketball.

The early high school coaches were Homer Christensen, Stubby Peterson and Pesty Jarvis. Then, in 1921, a man who had been a star player at Utah State Agricultural College in Logan—Tommy H. McMullin—took over and became a legend in basketball as Santistevan became in football and baseball.

McMullin also coached football for two years and one of his star players was John Vranes who later coached at Jordan and West. But it was basketball that endeared Tommy to all Binghamites.

On his first team in 1921, Tommy had two great stars in Lawrence "Tuffy" Stillman and Adolph Chiara.

"Stillman, for his day, had no equal," Tommy said recently. "He could do it all—shoot, pass, dribble, play defense. He was a superb performer. He was the very best."

In the following 13 years, Tommy took Bingham to the state basketball tournament 12 times. "We were always after the championship, but we couldn't make it. Something always happened to us," Tommy said.

Among the players were such stars as Bryan Thomas, Jim Siddoway, Harold "Fat" Williams, John Dahlstrom, Tommy Wilson, Porta Olias, Eddie Grant, Lyle Brady, Alvin Hall, Ole Hervilla, Steve Vlasic, Walt Bolic, Pete Pitchos, Hugo Bianchi, George Knudsen and Elmer Knudsen.

Pitchos later became sheriff of Los Angeles County. Hall was a sports and civic leader in Bingham, and Hervilla moved to California where he became a real estate millionaire.

Playing in the old gymnasium had a built-in advantage. The floor was on the third floor of the building. It was small and had a circular track above it that cut off the corners of the playing floor.

"The track was just like having an extra guard," Tommy recalls. "We didn't lose too many games on that floor."

The gym was small and it was always packed for the Miners' games. And the fans had a special halftime show of their own. Young boys would get into the games and lie under the bleacher seats peering at the game through the legs of seated customers. At halftime the lights would be turned out and the fans would toss coins onto the floor. The boys would scramble out from under the stands and pick up the coins when the lights came on.

When the high school was moved to Copperton in 1931, there was a lot of opposition in Bingham, especially over having the gym out of town. But the new high school had a spacious gym and eventually the opposition was won over.

To go to the tournament 12 of 13 years, the Miners had to win their division title or finish second each year, but in the new gym the tide turned and Bingham went several years without reaching the tournament. After the 1936 season, Tommy resigned to devote full time to his duties as principal and Warren "Sunny" Allsop, another Utah State Agricultural College great, took his place.

Allsop coached the Miners to second place in the 1951 State Class B tournament in the old University of Utah field-house. In the championship game the Miners lost to Monroe in overtime, 42-40.

Playing for Bingham that year were Ed Gaythwaite, Bob Sanchez, Richard Allsop (Sunny's son), Chris Ballamis, Ray Hall, John Erickson, "Bullet" Goris, Albert Gallegos.

So, the state basketball championship, a dream of every Binghamite, escaped Allsop just as it had McMullin. But the Miners had some great players over those years including Jack Knudsen, Kenny Hall, Billy Thomas, Chris Apostol, Kent Stillman (Tuffy Stillman's son), Jimmy Bernardo, Howie Hausknecht, Sergio Alvarez, Emil Pollick and Dean Stringham.

Sanchez later coached Murray High School and then became principal at Morgan High School. Stringham played at Utah State then coached football at Tooele and Brighton High Schools.

When Allsop stepped down after the 1953 season, another former Aggie took his place. Udell Wankier became Bingham's third basketball coach since 1921, and he was to be a big winner.

In 1954, the Miners took consolation honors in the state tournament, but didn't make the tournament in 1955, the senior year of one of the school's all-time great players, Jack Mannion. Mannion was sensational and was named all-state without reaching the tourament, almost unheard of in Utah history.

From 1956, through 1964, Bingham went to the state tournament every year and in 1960, finally realized the dream of winning a state championship.

But first there were to be two close calls.

In 1956, the Miners reached the finals only to lose to Pleasant Grove, 61-56. Ironically, Pleasant Grove was coached by a former Bingham athlete, Don Crump.

Playing for Bingham on that 1956 team were Mike Gonzales, Ron Boren, Joe Castillo, George Rekoutis, Jerry Crellin, Dick Susaeta, Robert King, Robert Nickolls, Jim Fike, Tim Leonard, Tom Lovat and Dave Cunliffe.

The next year, 1957, Bingham swept through its entire pre-season and season schedule without a loss and went to the tournament in the BYU fieldhouse. There they went through the first three games and went into the championship game with Panguitch undefeated.

But in that title game the old jinx held and Bingham lost, 49 to 45.

Castillo, Rekoutis, Lovat, Leonard and Nickolls were back from the 1966 team and the other members were, Larry

Dahlin, Norman Bianchi, Bob Davis, Eddie Garamendi, Joe Robertson, Boyd Whetzel and Bill English.

In 1958, Bingham became a Class A school and went to the A tournament in 1958, 1959, and then came 1960.

This was Bingham's year of destiny, although for many it came too late. Bingham won the state Class A basketball championship by beating Olympus in the title game, 64 to 53.

The championship team was led by the sons of two former Bingham athletic greats. Guard Johnny Johnson was the son of Bill Johnson who was a great shortstop for Gemmell Club, and George Sluga, a forward, was the son of George Sluga, another Gemmell Club great as a pitcher and hitter.

Other starters were Dave Erickson, Harold Dimond and Roy Hatch. The rest of the team included, Grant Price, Jimmy Lovat, Clifford Butt, Paul Weichman, Kent Simpkins, Reeves Dahlstrom, John Ugarte and Frank Dimond.

The official celebration honoring the champions was held in the Civic Center in Bingham Canyon under the direction of Principal Joel Jensen. So, the old gym did get a chance to feel the feet of a state championship team.

It was a great moment, but the town was already decimated and the celebration was nothing compared to what it would have been had it come 10, 20 or 30 years earlier.

Bingham reached the A semifinals in 1963, and the team stars were guards Jim Jimas and Randy Schouten. Both players went on to star at BYU where Jimas became one of the top college players in the region.

In 1968, Bingham went to the tournament again with Wayne Steadman, Paul Harker and Steve McKee the stars.

After that season Wankier left to take the head job at the new Brighton High School and George Sluga, who had starred on that state championship team of 1960, replaced him.

In high school tennis, Bingham's best player was generally regarded to be John Curry who played in 1939, '40 and '41. Curry teamed with Jack Edwards to give the Miners a strong doubles team and following their graduation, Steve Pickering became the star. Earlier, Les and Tom Carrigan were tennis stars.

Maureen Jensen, playing in the early 1940's, was an exceptional player and had girls been allowed to compete on the boys' teams in those years, she might easily have lettered in tennis.

But the high school teams were not the only teams in Bingham Canyon.

When Copperton was built in the 1920's, the Copper Ball Park was also built there. The park had a high board fence completely surrounding it. There were first and third base bleachers and a covered grandstand with a small press box on top, and two concession stands.

There the early baseball teams in the old Copper League competed in a kind of intra-mural competition. Then the Gemmell Club team and the Apex and U.S. Mine teams played in the Copper League and the Industrial League.

Going to the Gemmell Club, Apex or U.S. Mines games were big events in the 1920's, '30's, and '40's. The games were usually played on Wednesdays and Sundays and the town of Bingham would empty for the games, the cars forming a long line to and from Copperton. On the way back up the canyon after a game, fans who had stayed home would call out to those returning for the score, and the result was always shouted back.

The Gemmell Club team reached the height of its popularity under the managership of peppery little Al Ablett who managed the clubhouse and the team.

Ablett became famous for his charges from the dugout to home plate for an argument with the umpire. Ablett would shout "Holy Cow" and away he would run. He also wrote a sports column for the *Bingham Bulletin,* served as an umpire and was active in civic affairs.

Darrell Kidd and Charley Bates were leading umpires and favorites with Binghamites.

On baseball days, the Utah Copper Mine would close at 3:30 P.M. and this made them almost seem like holidays.

Among the players who performed in the Copper Park were catchers, Red Muir, Sparky Lawrence, Frank LaComb, Bus Smith, Bill Butler, Swede Johnson and Daryl Robertson; pitchers, Bill McIvor, Dusty Rhoades, Jerry Dunn, Whitey Cooper, Pee Wee Bass, Clair Johnson, Luis Valdez, Don Harrison, Sammy Oliver, Frank Shephard, Daka Davis and Tom Kelly; first basemen, Jack Smith, Charles Ames; second basemen, Doty Bush, Skinny Moore, Johnny Pearson; shortstop, Billy Johnson, Herb Babcock, Sparky Fielder; third basemen, Bailey Santistevan, Johnny Norek, Joe Myers; outfielders, Del Madsen, Les Sumnicht, Al Kastellic, Frank Zaccaria, Pete Hepting, George Sluga, Ug Wilson, Arn Valcheck, Spud Morley and Adolph Chiara.

In 1948, a Bingham town team sponsored by the Bingham District Athletic Association with Alvin Hall as president and coached by Les Sumnicht, won the Utah State Amateur championship. The team was comprised entirely of Bingham High School players or graduates.

The old Copper Ball Park also played another role in the life of the community. It was the home of the Eskimo Pie League.

The Eskimo Pie League was Bailey Santistevan's dream child and was a predecessor to today's boys' baseball programs.

It was open to every boy from 6 to 16. The younger boys had a pee wee softball program and the 9 to 16 age group played baseball. It was a superb league. The boys and Santistevan did everything themselves. No parents were involved. In fact, the only time the parents showed up there was during the annual Parent's Day when they visited as spectators.

The boys organized their own teams and obtained business sponsors who furnished them with baseball caps. The baseballs and bats were supplied by Santistevan and the boys spent hours sewing up old baseballs for the league.

A bus made the trip from Copperfield and Highland Boy to Copperton each weekday morning picking up the boys who hadn't already hitched a ride to the park.

The boys did everything. They kept their own score, had their own manager, did their own umpiring. When a dispute arose, Santistevan was the final word. Many games would be played at the same time in the park and a runner might slide home, be called safe, and an argument arise in one end of the park while Santistevan was at the opposite end with his back turned. But the teams involved would each send a representative to Santistevan who would listen, then rule "safe" or "out," and that was that. There was no appeal.

Bingham Canyon held many boxing and wrestling programs in the Gemmell Club and Civic Center, and on these cards, the boys of the town usually furnished some of the competition with fans throwing money into the ring after such bouts.

Gemmell Club also had a basketball team in the semipro Industrial League in the 1930's, and early '40's. Allsop and A. J. Boberg coached the team and it had such players as Shelby West, Marlowe Turpin, Neil Carroll, Dick Marsh, Herb Babcock, Frank Hunter, Frank Stepan, Hugo Bianchi, Steve Pazell, Bob Burke, Bob Davis and Bob Dettmer.

There were only two bowling lanes in the basement of the Gemmell Club but the town produced some of Utah's greatest names in bowling.

Ann Pechina, whose family home was destroyed in the Highland Boy fire, married a Salt Laker, Bob Slattery, and as Ann Slattery won the United States Women's All-Star Bowling Championship in 1965.

Ann is the only Utah bowler to win a national title.

But among the top men bowlers over the years have been Binghamites, Frank Zaccaria, George Sluga, Kenny Chestnut, Peppy Borich, Russell Boren, Gus Katis, John Kallen, Wee Lopez, Al Ablett, Bill Ablett, Pete Yano (who owned the State Lanes in Salt Lake), Jerry Dunn, Warren "Sunny" Allsop, who is a director of the Salt Lake City Bowling Association, Jim Abplanalp, Mickey Callisto, Max Sluga, George Abplanalp and Kenneth Reid.

CHAPTER EIGHT

ALL THE MEN WERE BIG MEN

IT WAS A HOT July night in the summer of 1971, and everyone came late. The meeting was to have started at 7:30 P.M. but it was 8 o'clock before everyone arrived in the court room on the second floor of the City Hall in Bingham Canyon.

Mayor Peter C. Dimas was in charge. Councilmen Gail Farnsworth, James Xanthos and Evelyn Fontana were there along with Clerk Mae Stillman. Kennecott Copper Corporation had a representative and Salt Lake attorney Robert S. Campbell Jr., who had been retained to represent both the town and Xanthos, was there.

On March 16, Kennecott had filed two civil suits against the town and Xanthos. The suits asked for condemnation of the City Hall, a section of Main Street and the fire station; Xantho's souvenir shop, the Tourist Center; and sought immediate occupancy of the property.

Kennecott stated in the complaint that a railroad track and roadways crossing property owned by the city of Bingham Canyon must be relocated and that Utah law gives Kennecott the power of eminent domain if necessary to maintain the mining operation.

It stated the work would provide the most public good and the least private injury to all concerned. The company said it would turn over a fire station it owned to the city and that another building would be made available for use as City Hall.

Judge Jeppson denied the motion for condemnation of the property and immediate occupancy, but made no ruling on the company's claim to eminent domain. He set trial for September 20.

And now, in July, the company representative at the meeting asked the council to settle the issue peaceably. It would have been easy. The company already had an option to purchase the Dimas and Fontana properties. There were only 19 people still living in the canyon. Councilman Farnsworth had already sold and was moving out. Xanthos was the only owner whose private property was involved. The board members could have sold the city property and pulled out of the fight.

And this July meeting would decide that question. The right of Xanthos to sit on the council was questioned. It was mentioned that he had a conflict of interest and was asked to take himself out of the discussion.

"I won't remove myself, but if the others on the board think I should be removed, they can do it," Xanthos said.

It was a dramatic moment, but the board held firm and said Xanthos would be involved in any decision of the board.

Then Mrs. Fontana took the floor. "As long as one small human being in the canyon needs the service of the City Council, that is where I owe my responsibility," she said.

There was no peace settlement. The case that would decide whether Bingham Canyon would die in condemnation by a private company, or would have the right to decide its own fate, would go to trial in the fall.

Pete Dimas, James Xanthos and Evelyn Klonizos Fontana had become the central figures in the final drama involving Bingham Canyon's life as a town. All three were of Greek ancestry with fathers who had been respected small businessmen in the community. All three were born in the canyon and grew up there at a time when the city was at the height of its power. And all three had watched it wither away.

The end of Bingham Canyon would come on November 22 of that year. But the issue now was, how would that end come?

Bingham Canyon was a young town, but she had aged rapidly in the last ten years.

Expansion of its open pit mine was essential and Kennecott Copper Corporation began buying property around the canyon as it became available for some time prior to 1959. And, property became more and more available through the 1950's. Shortly after the middle of the year in 1959, a long strike began against Kennecott, more families left the area and as the year dragged toward a close the handwriting went on the wall.

On December 7, 1959, 175 of the 179 property owners in Bingham Canyon met and named a central committee to meet with Kennecott officials and discuss possible sale of the city. Boyd J. Nerdin was named chairman of the committee.

On February 18, 1960, the property owners' committee met with company officials and were asked to come up with a figure for complete sale of the city. The Kennecott representatives indicated that if the amount was right, purchase of all homes, buildings and grounds would be considered.

A week later, at 7:30 P.M. on Wednesday, February 14, 1960, 275 Bingham Canyon residents met with the committee in the Princess Theater and were asked to arrive at an aggregate total price to present to Kennecott for consideration.

Nerdin asked property owners to be realistic in appraising their property, but said some provision should be made for "intrinsic value."

"We don't expect the company to accept our figure. In fact, we know of four pieces of property which they have appraised just this week," Nerdin said.

Someone in the audience asked if it would be possible to sell and then rent the house back and continue living in the canyon? "No!" Nerdin answered. "Once they've bought the town we get out. They've told us they are not in the real estate business."

Harold F. Chesler, justice of the peace and a committee member, reminded everyone that Kennecott could spot buy piece-by-piece thus depreciating remaining properties.

Wally Swenson, who lived at 276 Main Street, dissented. "Why," he asked, "should we sell our homes for a song, move to the valley and go into debt 20 years?"

Fire Chief John Creedon pointed out the fact that many persons there had their roots pretty deep in Bingham and would be reluctant to leave.

There was evidence that Kennecott, too, might be reluctant. In its final paragraph in the story reporting the meeting, the *Deseret News* said: "Kennecott officials have informed the committee that future mine engineering plans do not include expansion into city property but that if citizens were anxious to sell, the company would consider an offer."

A standing vote was taken authorizing the committee to continue negotiations with the company.

But, very little came of the joint effort and it dissipated.

On July 8, 1960, the Bingham Businessmen's Association announced it was sponsoring a drive to refill empty apartments and build up the city.

After stating that he felt the negotiations to sell the city were at a stalemate, Kimball Goff, association president, announced that a meeting would be held July 27, at 1 P.M. in the City Hall for home and apartment owners and people who would like to rent in Bingham.

"Many people left after it was announced that negotiations had started to sell the property to Kennecott Copper Corporation. People left because they felt they would have to move in the near future.

"However, with the negotiations at a stalemate many have indicated a desire to return," Goff said.

In listing advantages to living in Bingham, Goff pointed out the fact that garbage collection was free, water cost was $1 per month, rent was low and it was close to work.

A few people did return, but it was not enough. The people were leaving, not returning.

Landmarks vanished. The Cyprus Hall was razed. The Princess Theater closed. The library, which had moved from the City Hall to a big building on Main Street, closed. Fire destroyed four homes in Markham Gulch. The Diamond Bar was torn down. Apartment houses were torn down or stood empty. The end, it appeared, could not be more than a year or two away.

By August 4, 1961, Union Drug had moved to Lead Mine and Centre Market to Copperton. Bingham Central was closed but still standing. The City Hall, Dimas' Grocery Store, the Midway Garage, the bank, UP&L, the post office, the fire halls, Civic Center, four taverns and the Tourist Center were still open. There were still some residences occupied.

Ed Brentel, who lived at 339 Main Street, summed up the feelings of those people still living there when he told a reporter, "I was born here, went to Italy for awhile, but came back 35 years ago. I'd stay permanently if they'd let me. It's cheaper living. It's cool up here, nobody bothers you. I hate to see the town go."

But go it did.

In 1962, Joe Dispenza ended eight years of service as mayor and Peter C. Dimas was elected in his place. He would serve in that post continuously until the end.

On January 4, 1962, *The Deseret News* reported a meeting of the Jordan School District in Sandy which was attended by J. P. O'Keefe, general manager of Kennecott Copper Corporation. The meeting opened negotiations between Kennecott and the school board for purchase of Bingham Central School.

In part the story said:

"In answer to a question by the board, Mr. O'Keefe emphasized that the buying of the Bingham property in the last couple of years was an idea that originated with the local property owners and not with the company.

" 'We have no possible use for the property. The residents came and made their request. The pit is not going to be moved down there (into town)' the KCC official said.

" 'We don't want to use it,' he said in referring to the school building constructed in 1924. 'If we buy it, it will just be torn down.'

"He said some parts of Bingham had been purchased in years before 1959, for use in connection with the company operation.

" 'This shrinkage, the inconvenience of continual blasting in the immediate vicinity, and other factors, apparently led the property owners to ask the company to buy their holdings,' Mr. O'Keefe told the board.

" 'Bingham has been deteriorating rather badly over the last 25 years,' he said.

" 'It's a tough place to live and a tough place to bring up children. There was a time when the workers had to live close to the mine. With modern transportation, it's not necessary any more,' Mr. O'Keefe said.

"Appraisals have been made of the school property. The school board took the proposal under advisement and told the delegation of KCC officials that it would reach a decision in the near future."

On March 24, 1962, the Bingham Central School was razed as part of a program by Kennecott Copper Corporation to remove structures from the ground it had purchased in the canyon.

Copperfield and Highland Boy went and in 1965, Kennecott and Anaconda Copper joined in a petition to disconnect all their properties from Bingham's incorporated area. A. J. Thuli, chief engineer of Utah Copper Division, Kennecott Copper Corporation, told an audience of about 20 persons in a meeting in Bingham that the company wanted residents to know of the action. He said that Kennecott Copper was disconnecting because the corporation no longer needs or desires services by Bingham City.

The Third District Court granted the petition and Bingham City appealed, but the Utah Supreme Court sustained the ruling in a unanimous decision.

In fighting the petition, Bingham officials argued in court it would cost the township $28,000 annually in sales and use of taxes distributed by Salt Lake County.

Supreme Court Justice Roger I. McDonough observed: "It is interesting to note that the city has a surplus in its treasury of $98,000 and there is little likelihood that any property tax would be levied against the city property owners in the near future."

Justice McDonough wrote that the property in question holds no dwellings, no inhabitants, "and there is no reasonable prospect of any such use in the future."

The ruling shrunk Bingham's boundaries from about 324 acres to 30 acres, and cut the town's revenues by 70 percent.

From September of 1960, until July, 1966, Kennecott made more than 200 purchases in the canyon. But in 1965, only three property owners sold to the company and by July of 1966, not one had sold in that year. So, Kennecott wrote a letter of ultimatum to 17 home and two business owners to sell by August 15, 1966, or lose the purchase prices offered by the company.

Still many held out.

Among these were Dimas, Xanthos and Mrs. Fontana. Dimas had closed down his grocery store as the population dwindled past the point it could be supported, but commuted to his outside job.

Mrs. Fontana was employed by Kennecott as part of the janitorial staff in Bingham, and Xanthos worked in Kennecott's machine shop in addition to running his souvenir shop on Main Street just below the City Hall.

A 1946 graduate of Bingham High School, Xanthos became interested in the souvenir business in 1955, and by 1957 had a steady business going.

Now, when almost everyone else was leaving, he was bringing in carloads of paint and material to maintain his Tourist Center, and he kept it stocked with a heavy inventory. He was getting ready for the summer tourist season when Kennecott filed its suit in March, 1971.

On September 1, 1971, a petition was filed in Third District Court to disincorporate the town. Only 19 people still lived in the city, 13 of them registered voters, and the petition asked the question be voted on in the November 2 election.

On September 2, Third District Judge Stewart M. Hanson signed an order directing that the city council place on the ballot the question of disincorporation.

On September 8, Bingham voters filed a counter petition in Third District Court protesting the earlier petition. The new petition, signed by two-thirds of the city's 13 qualified voters, stated the petition to disincorporate the City of Bingham "is harmful and contradictory to the case of Kennecott Copper Corporation vs. the City of Bingham."

And so the trial opened on Monday, September 20, 1971, in the court of Third District Judge D. Frank Wilkins.

The only witness the first day was Kenneth H. Matheson Jr., mining engineer for the open pit operation. He said the City Hall, fire station and souvenir shop were tying up an estimated 3.8 million tons of copper ore on the mine's north side. He said Kennecott must move a rail yard at the 6,190-foot level to get at the new ore. Moving the rail yard again in 1975 or 1976, would open up another six million tons of ore, he added.

Matheson said expansion was programmed in the firm's mining plans and money had been approved for the purchase. He said the expansion was impossible without the contested land.

The eminent domain law—subparagraph six of section 78-34-1 of the Utah Code—says the right to take private property for public use may be exercised for "roads, railroads, tunnels . . . and dumping places to facilitate the . . . working of mines. . . ."

Earlier court rulings decided that mining is a public use and "the right of eminent domain may be applied with full force and effect."

But the town's attorneys, Campbell and Stewart M. Hansen Jr., contended that Kennecott must show a need before authority to condemn the property could be obtained. They said Kennecott had other "viable alternatives" to accomplish its means. The lawyers also questioned the earlier rulings giving mining the right of eminent domain.

The second day of the trial lasted about 90 minutes before Judge Wilkins recessed court and moved into chambers with counsel for both sides to discuss the case.

Then, on Wednesday, September 22, the case was settled. Kennecott agreed to pay $313,800 for the three pieces of property it had sought to condemn. The settlement awarded $73,800 to the city for the City Hall, fire station and section of Main Street, and settled with the Xanthos family for the tourist center.

Under terms of the agreement with the city, Kennecott agreed to make its payment within 10 days and the city agreed to deed the property and vacate the street. All facilities were to be made available for January 1, 1972, occupancy. Kennecott agreed to let the city use the old post office (which it owned) to house the city government until another site could be obtained.

The court did not rule on Kennecott's "power or intitlement" to condemn property under Utah's eminent domain law, which formed the basis for the suit.

On November 2, the 13 voters in Bingham Canyon cast their ballots 11-2 in favor of disincorporation while electing Xanthos, Gladys Farnsworth and Mrs. Peter C. Dimas to the city council.

Mrs. Fontana, as clerk, submitted the election results to Salt Lake County on November 9.

The last residents in Bingham Canyon when it was still a town were Mr. and Mrs. Jim Aspiazu, Mrs. Rita Ugarte,

Mr. and Mrs. Peter C. Dimas and family, James Xanthos, Louie Panos, Mrs. Evelyn Fontana and her three sons, Mr. and Mrs. Gail Farnsworth, and Mrs. Marian Prigmore and family.

So, the town of Bingham Canyon ceased to exist although there were still some official matters to be disposed of and the council continued to meet in the old post office.

At one of the last meetings in the post office, a visitor and a tourist (who saw the doors open and just walked in) stood with Mayor Dimas and looked at a curious relic that had been removed from the City Hall and was stored in the post office before being transferred to someone's private collection.

It was a gigantic thing. The tourist looked at it, shook his head admiringly, and said: "From the looks of that, the men of Bingham Canyon must all have been very big men."

It was the old porcelain urinal that had hung in the men's room of the City Hall for so very many years.

Adios Amigo.

EPILOGUE

Now Bingham Canyon is gone. Nothing remains. She exists only in the memories of those who knew her when. How do you say goodbye to an old friend?

Just Adios Amigo? Like that?

No. Not that. That's too final. There must be no finality in the farewell. There must be hope that maybe someday, someway. . . .

Wait. Back in 1939, Bingham Canyon celebrated its first Galena Days. It was a holiday in which the old days were honored. It was an attempt to recapture the spirit of the past. It was an attempt to remember what the town had been like in a more carefree time.

Dale Johnston was general chairman of the first Galena Days celebration. He put his feelings for the event on paper. He wrote a poem that was published in the *Bingham Bulletin* on September 29, 1939. It was entitled, "Out of The Past."

'Tis midnight and the light of day
  Has long since disappeared.
The autumn moon there on the ridge,
  Casts shadows, long and weird.
The restless breeze goes scurrying
  Along the narrow street.
Another sound now fills the night—
  The tramp of ghostly feet!

Just now I heard a ghostly word,
A ghostly burro bray—
The mountain men are home again
To spend the holidays!
The canyon walls are echoing.
Once more to song and laughter.
A challenge flung from ghostly lips
To us who follow after—
"And shall you turn the challenge down
And hurry home to bed?
For who has most to celebrate—
The living or the dead?
Tonight once more from swinging doors
The yellow lamplight plays—
The mountain men are home again
To spend the holidays!
"What is the difference now from then?
This is the same old town!
The same old hills loom black above,
The same old moon looks down!
What if our strident voices are
But whispers in the dust?
We've come to celebrate!" they cry—
"Who's here to welcome us?"
A score of ghostly shouts ring out
From a bar across the way.
The mountain men are home again
To spend Galena Days.

DEE JOHANSON COLLECTION

Dry Fork with English Dairy corral, barns on left, residence on right.

DEE JOHANSON COLLECTION

This picture was taken on trail that circled from Heaston Heights to Freeman Gulch. It shows Frogtown, Railroad Avenue, Freeman Gulch, Dixon Gulch and Hegland Alley. The George E. Chandler mansion with its back yard and fence borders Hegland Alley.

Main Street just below Heaston Heights, November 29, 1937.

MRS. C. A. DUNN COLLECTION

Heaston Heights in 1928. It changed little over the years.

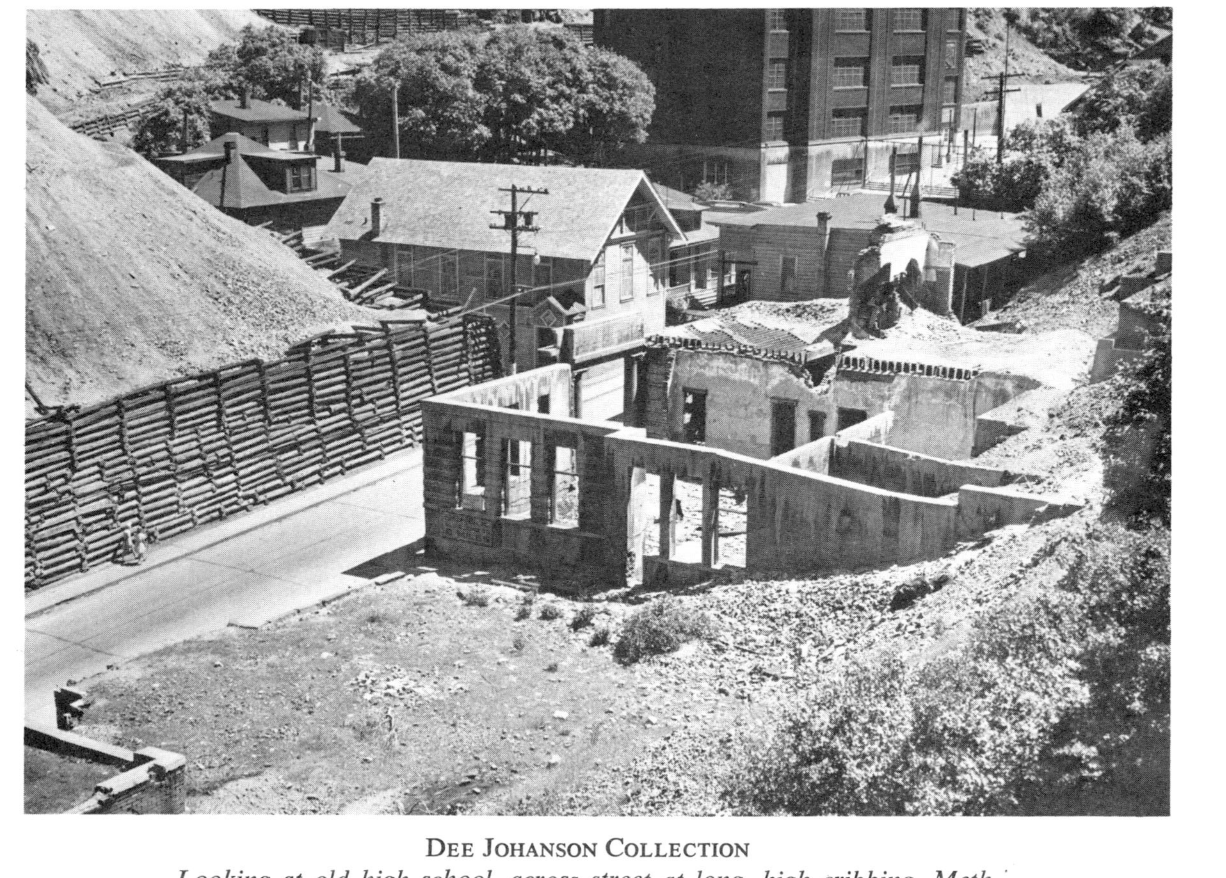

DEE JOHANSON COLLECTION

Looking at old high school, across street at long, high cribbing, Methodist Church, McGuire Gulch and Bingham Central School.

DEE JOHANSON COLLECTION

Looking down Markham Gulch. Canyon Hall is big building on front left of gulch. Across street is Bingham Central School and playground. Building on opposite hill at left is UP&L substation.

DEE JOHANSON COLLECTION

This is view looking up canyon from high on hillside of Markham Gulch. First building at lower left is Chipian's store. The view is of entire section of Main Street from Markham up to where it turned toward Copperfield in summer of 1936.

School children parade down business district. Bourgard Apartments are on left.

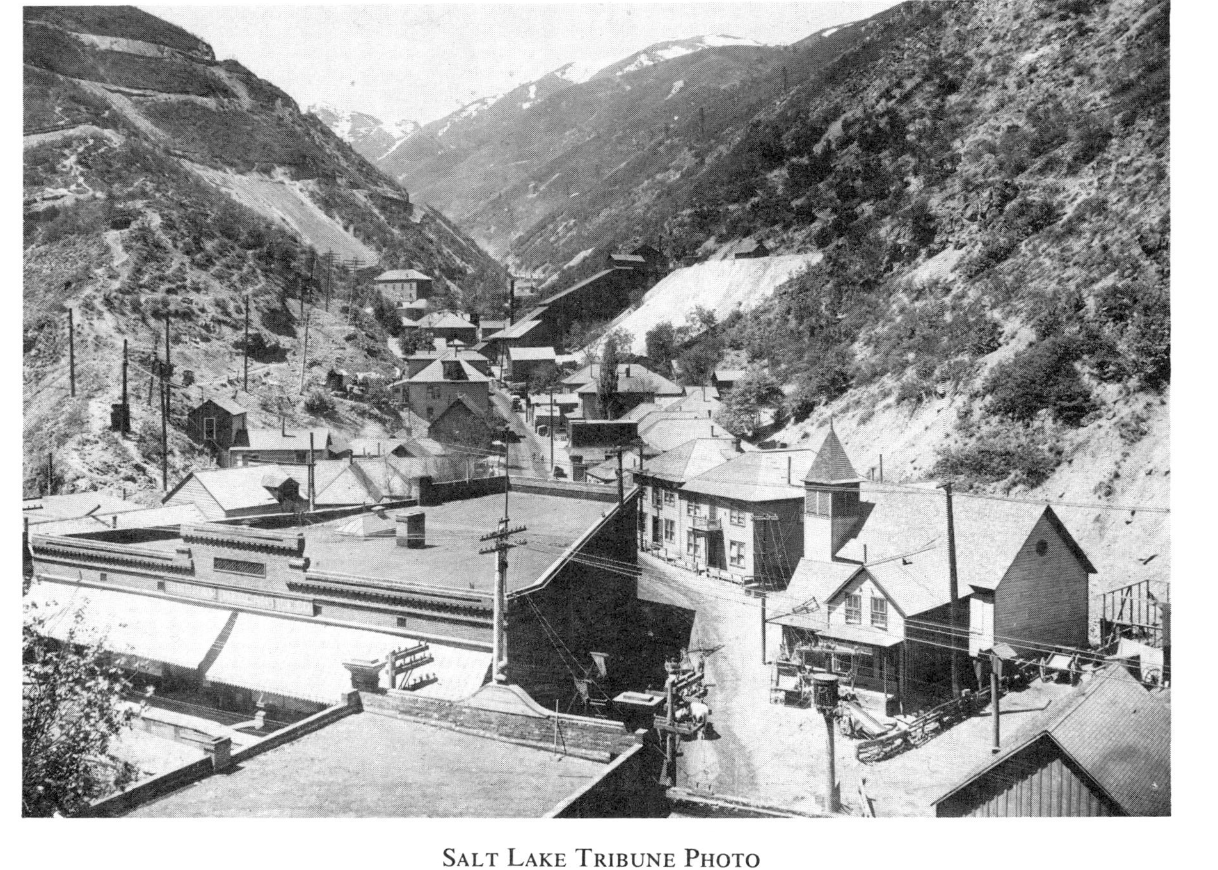

Salt Lake Tribune Photo

This picture of Bingham Mercantile corner, Main Street and Carr Fork

Carr Fork in 1920.

SALT LAKE TRIBUNE PHOTO

Looking down canyon from Highland Boy in July, 1939.

Upper Main Street as it looked on September 10, 1940.

Highland Boy in early 1900's.

BINGHAM LIONS CLUB PHOTO

One of famous landmarks in Copperfield. The spectacular E Line Bridge.

Copperfield before the vehicular tunnel was built.

DEE JOHANSON COLLECTION
Greek Camp in Copperfield.

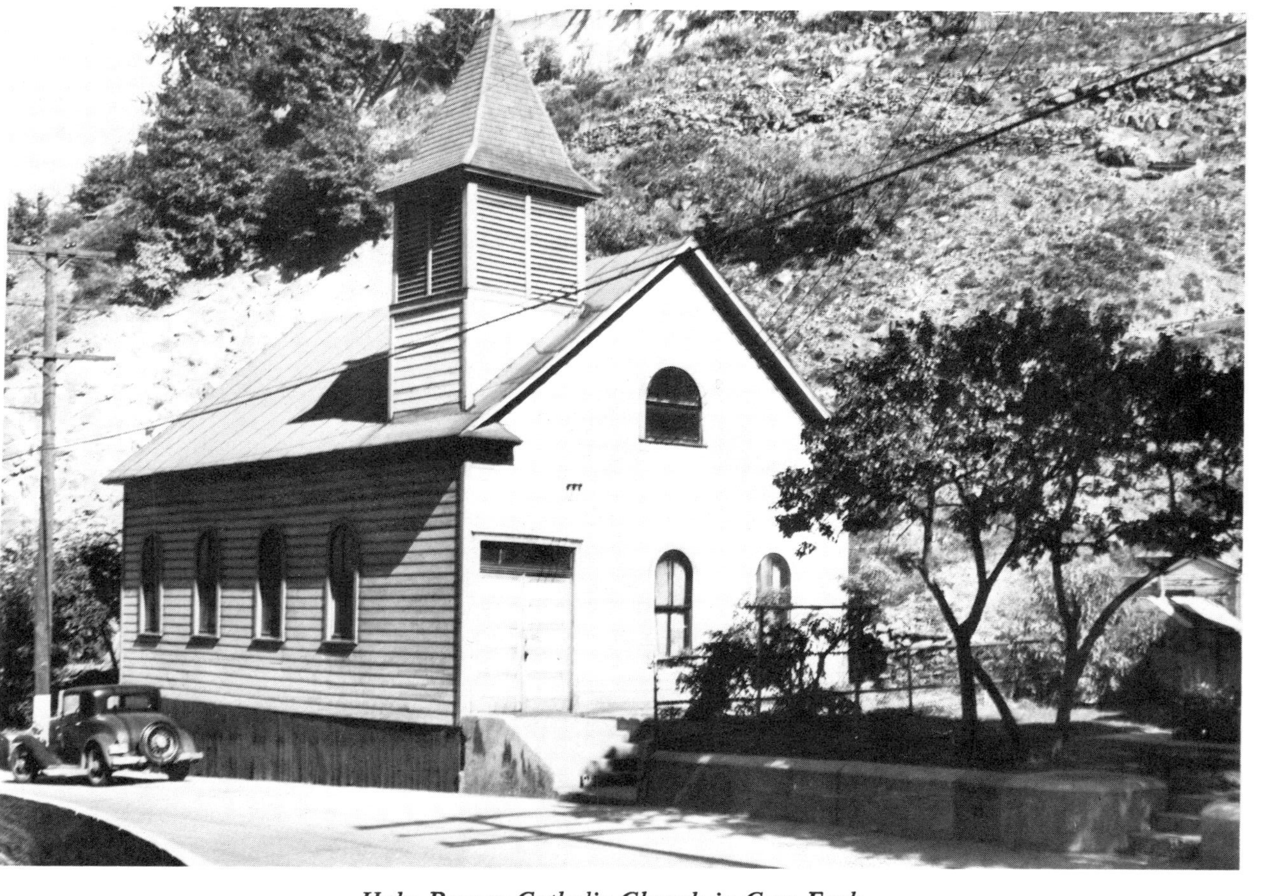

Holy Rosary Catholic Church in Carr Fork.

Highland Boy's Community House.

The Methodist Church on Main Street and McGuire Gulch.

Wolfe's Yard area in Frogtown in 1937.

D&RG Depot on Railroad Avenue in 1936. Creek is on left of tracks.

The Utah Copper Clinic where Dr. Russell G. Frazier and Dr. Harold H. Jenkins had office. Dentist, Dr. B. D. Bennion, had office upstairs.

BOYD HOUSEHOLDER COLLECTION

Bingham's early firemen with trucks, equipment in front of Fire Hall No. 2.

A ward dinner in Bingham's LDS ward house.

Dee Johanson Collection

Early holiday in Bingham Canyon.

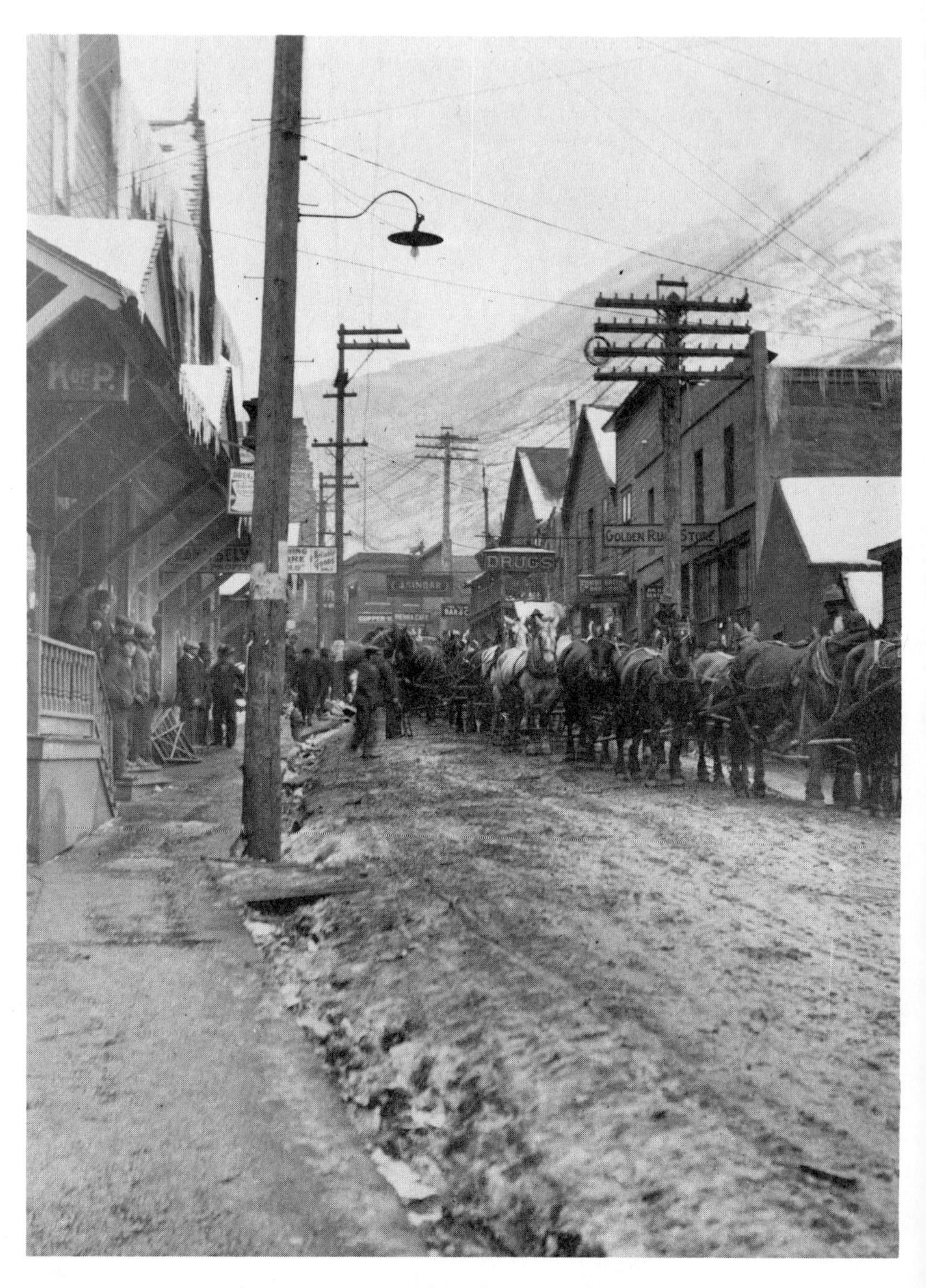

DEE JOHANSON COLLECTION

Horse teams haul ore wagons down canyon.

REX TRIPP COLLECTION

Main Street below Civic Center in early days of camp.

REX TRIPP COLLECTION
Upper Main Street in the spring of 1914.

Main Street with the Diamond Ring sign on right.

UTAH STATE HISTORICAL SOCIETY

The Griffin House, a hotel and boarding house, stood at corner of Main Street and Carr Fork where Bingham Mercantile was built later.

The front of telephone office in 1912 wnen it was located in basement of Bingham Merc building. Men are Bill Mitchell and manager Francis W. Quinn.

REX TRIPP COLLECTION

This early photo in canyon shows LDS ward house on hill at left. Heaston Heights area has no homes as yet and notice the creek running down the center of canyon floor. It was the town's sewer.

A Boy Scouts father and sons banquet in Bingham in 1924. Left to right: Andrew Contratto, Joe Toy, Bill Grant, Eddie Grant, Bob Miller, William Hull, R. C. Miller; Second row: Joe Berger, Dee Johanson, Harry Jordon, C. E. Adderley, Miles Hartman, Wesley Straup, Currey Leiser, Bill Trevarthen, Otto Carpenter, Bill Carpenter, Fritz Carpenter, W. J. Thomas, Carl Meyers, Arthur Jones, Mark Jones, Ed Heather, Jim Barkle, Riley Tatten, Bobby Wells, Dr. Russell G. Frazier, J. B. Meyers, J. W. Colyar.

The Tram in operation.

Rex Tripp Collection
Inside the Bingham Mercantile in early 1920's.

Ed Johnson Collection
Inside Bourgard's Butcher Shop in 1923.

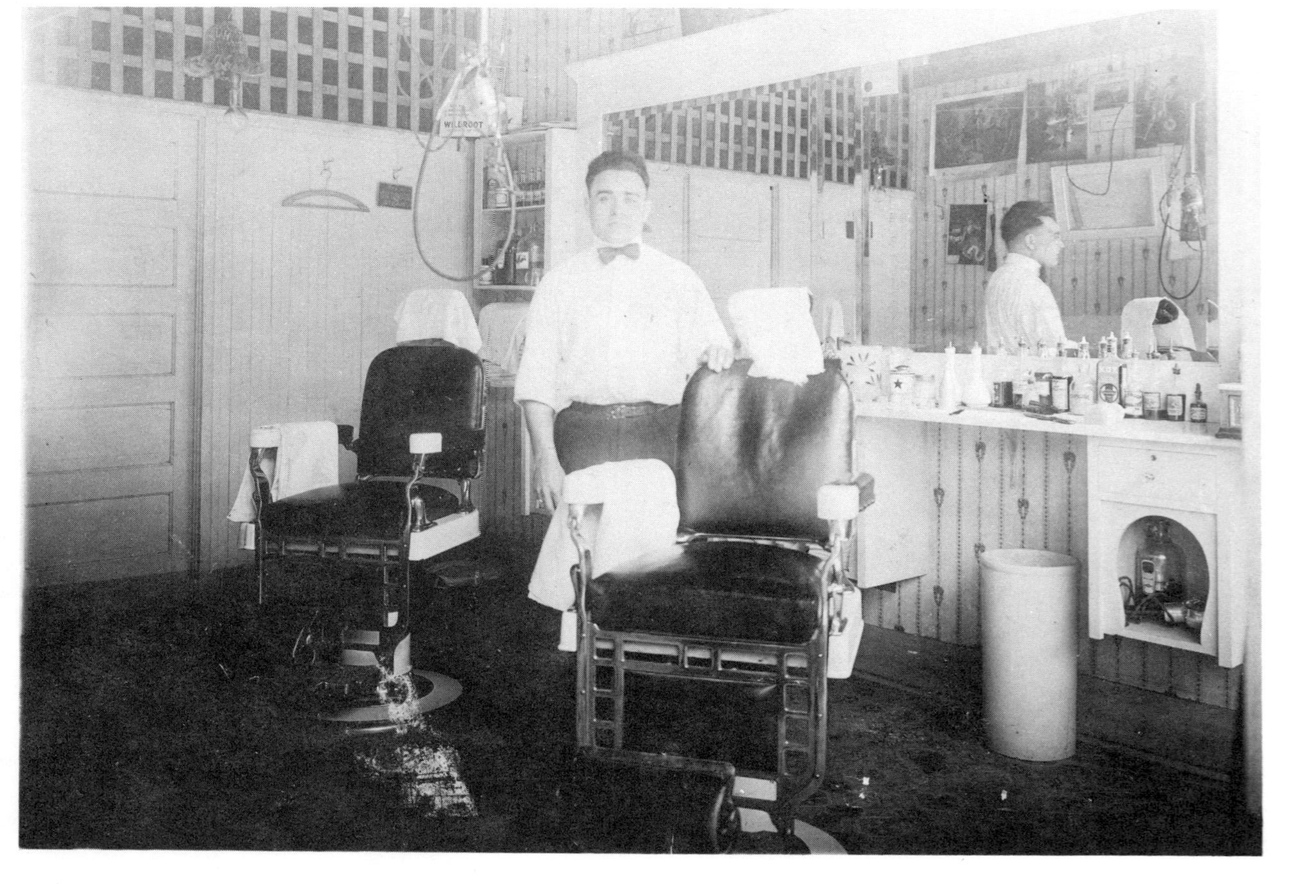

EVELYN FONTANA COLLECTION

George Klonzios in his barber shop at 19 Carr Fork.

UTAH STATE HISTORICAL SOCIETY
Highland Boy. The overhead Tram.

Bingham Lions Club Photo
Freeman Gulch in 1925.

DEE JOHANSON COLLECTION

Dr. Paul S. Richards and Bingham Hospital staff on patio behind hospital.

Highland Boy snowslide, 1939.

Highland Boy fire, 1932.

ED JOHNSON COLLECTION

Bingham residents put on own production of "Aunt Lucia" on stage of Princess Theater. Here the cast, comprised entirely of Binghamites, poses for group picture on stage of the theater, January 15, 1930.

Bingham holds street dance on Main Street as part of Galena Days celebration in 1939.

DEE JOHANSON COLLECTION
Bingham celebrates V-J Day.

One-time Bingham City officials Dr. F. E. Straup, and Charles E. Adderley talk over early struggles in city government.

Ed Johnson, who was born in 1893 and saw Bingham City through its entire career, was mayor in 1938 when Bingham became third class city. Here Mr. Johnson holds early mementos of town, a Bourgard Butcher Shop calendar for 1913, and a dance card from Canyon Hall in 1913.

Bingham High School's long-time principal Tommy H. McMullin.

Dr. Russell G. Frazier, Bingham physician, during his tour as senior medical officer with Admiral Byrd's expedition to Antarctic 1939-'41.

Galena Days traffic jam.

BINGHAM LIONS CLUB PHOTO

Fire on Main Street in early days of town.

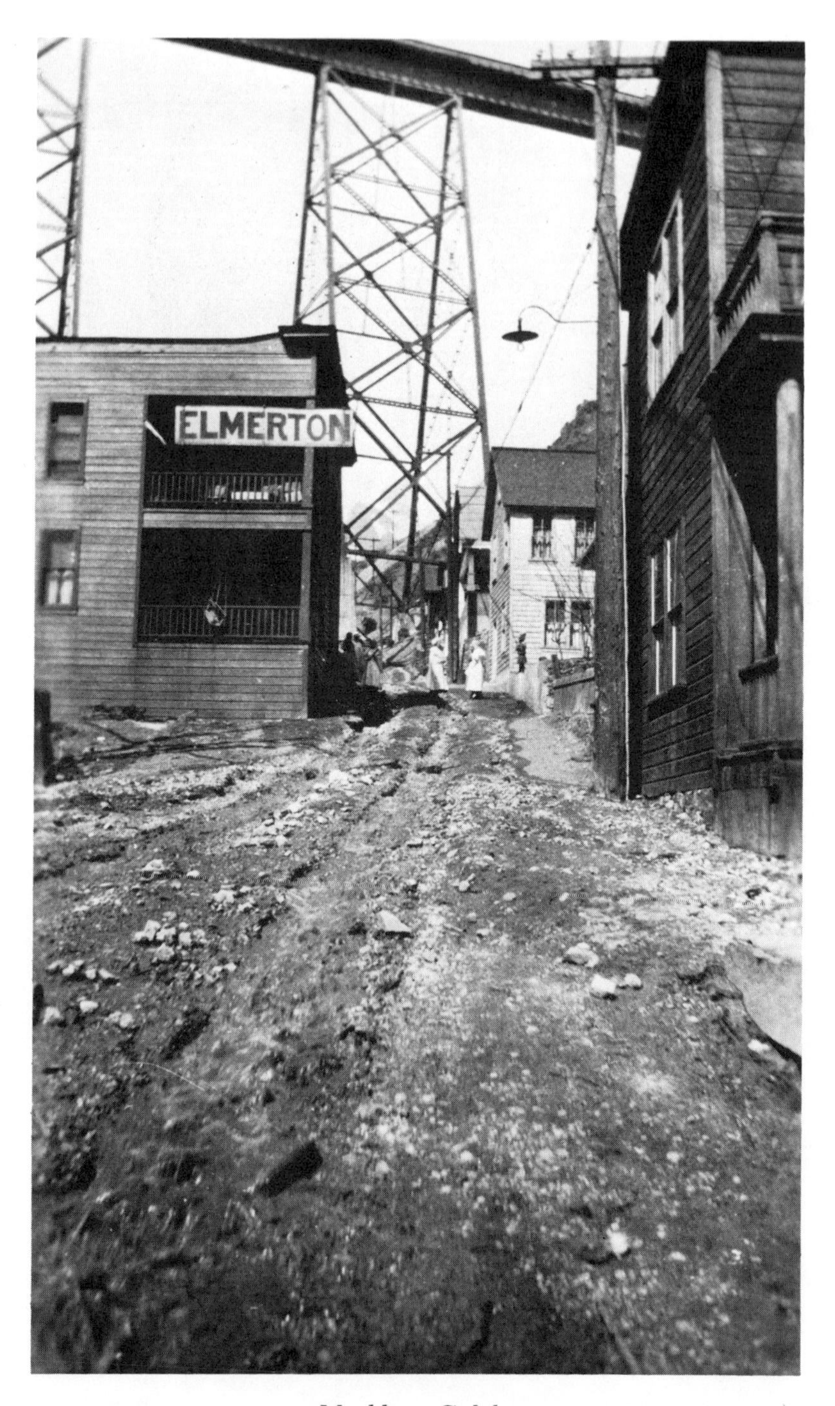

Markham Gulch

EDITH SANTISTEVAN COLLECTION

Bingham High School's last basketball team to play in old gym building, 1930-'31. Front row, left to right: Steve Vlasic, Kenny Harker, Les Carrigan, Walt Bolic, Panos Pitchos, Dan Churich, Mike Strelich, Angelo Pagnotta, Billy Johnson. Back row: assistant coach Bailey Santistevan, George Markovich, Clair Johnson, "Spike" Error, Victor Contratto, Lawrence Ray, Jack Smith, Paul Slotti, Mike Pazell, coach Tommy McMullin.

Three views of youth playing baseball in Eskimo Pie League in Copper Ball Park in 1930's.

REX TRIPP COLLECTION
The Lashbrook Store, first one in Bingham Canyon.

Dimas' Bingham Grocery just before being torn down.

Charles E. Adderley house (above) and two other winter scenes on same section of Main Street in 1930's. Just up canyon from Markham Gulch.

The Post Office: The steps leading to LDS ward house; and Bingham strongman Dave Wheret.

Commercial class types away in old high school in 1918.

Cast of Bingham High School play poses in the old gym in 1918. Notice circular track.

Bingham gets its Main Street paved in fall of 1928. It was a hard job many said couldn't be done. After street was closed three days, fire broke out and it had to be opened, but paving job was successful.

This picture was taken in front of the Apex Mercantile Co. building in Highland Boy showing the Serbian Lodge members in uniform in 1908. Joseph Melich is the second man from the right of the man holding the flag on the left. His wife, Mary, is on the balcony holding their son, Mitch. Mitch Melich grew up, became a lawyer, and millionaire in the uranium business in Moab as a partner with Charlie Steen. In 1964 Mitch Melich ran for Governor of Utah on the Republican ticket.